THE

Mount of Blessing;

OR,

LECTURES ON THE BEATITUDES.

BY

REV. GEORGE C. CRUM.

EDITED BY

REV. D. W. CLARK, D. D.

Cincinnati:
PUBLISHED BY L. SWORMSTEDT & A. POE,
FOR THE METHODIST EPISCOPAL CHURCH, AT THE WESTERN BOOK CONCERN,
CORNER OF MAIN AND EIGHTH STREETS.

R. P. THOMPSON, PRINTER.
1854.

TO

My Venerable and Beloved Father,

THESE

LECTURES ARE INSCRIBED,

AS A

SLIGHT TOKEN

OF

PROFOUND RESPECT AND FILIAL AFFECTION,

BY THE AUTHOR.

Recommendatory Notice.

By the courtesy of the author, Rev. George C. Crum, I have read, in manuscript, "The Mount of Blessing; or, Lectures on the Beatitudes," and take pleasure in expressing my decided approval of the work. The topics chosen are of vital importance in the formation of Christian character; the style is admirably adapted to the subject; the principles laid down are evangelical, and a spirit of heavenly sweetness is diffused throughout the whole. To all who seek "the path of life," as marked out by Him who is "the light of the world," these beautiful and instructive Lectures are cheerfully recommended by

T. A. Morris.

Cincinnati, April, 1854.

PREFACE.

Dear Friend,—Permit me to detain you a moment. The Lectures you are about to read are upon one of the most beautiful and interesting portions of Divine truth. The Beatitudes have ever been admired. They show us so much of the Savior's heart; they so graphically pencil the characters he loves; they unseal such a full and sweet fountain of comfort, that a pious mind can not fail to realize both pleasure and profit in meditating upon them. So peculiarly are they constructed, if I may thus speak, that they adapt themselves, in some degree, to every kind of temperament, to every stage of Christian experience, and every circumstance of human life. They delineate character, they prompt us to an effort of imitation, and pronounce a blessing upon every humble and sincere endeavor. Standing, as we seem to, around the Mount, under the uplifted hands of Jesus, while blessings, like the river of life, pour from his opening lips, our weakness should change to strength, our despair to joyful hope, and our tottering footsteps to a firm and rapid movement along the highway of holiness.

To expound and apply the truth as taught in this portion of our Lord's Sermon on the Mount, is the object of these Lectures. How far I have succeeded others must determine. They came up in the ordinary course of pulpit preparation, and were designed especially for those over whom I was set in the ministry of the word. They are the result of thought and prayer, and were written out at intervals and amidst deep personal affliction. The critical will find many imperfections; but friends, to whose judgment I would bow in other respects, have advised their publication; and hence their appearance in the present form. I send them forth to do good. Should they lead one soul to the Savior, or shed one ray of light upon a desponding heart, or in any degree advance the cause of my Redeemer, I have my reward.

GEO. C. CRUM.

Cincinnati, April, 1854.

CONTENTS.

LECTURE I.

The Mount of Blessing.

THE GREAT TEACHER.

"And seeing the multitudes, he went up into a mountain: and when he was set, his disciples came unto him. And he opened his mouth, and taught them." MATTHEW v, 1, 2.

THE Son of God had now entered the world. Prophecy had indicated, long before his advent, that he would be a prophet as well as a priest and king. "Thus Moses said unto the fathers, A prophet shall the Lord your God raise up unto you of your brethren, like unto me." In succeeding ages, other inspired seers had described him as a Teacher, a Wise Counselor, and the Messenger of the Covenant—forms of expression applicable to him only in the character of a teacher. The beautiful images of a star and a sun point him out as the source of intelligence, and show their propriety in those divine instructions which fell from his lips while he sojourned on the earth. A striking fulfillment of these ancient predictions is seen on the first Sabbath of his ministry. Being at Nazareth, "he entered into a synagogue, as his custom was, and opening the book of the prophet Esaias, read: The Spirit of the Lord is upon me, because the Lord hath anointed me to preach the Gospel to the poor; he hath sent me to heal the broken-hearted, to preach deliverance to the captives, and recovering of sight to the blind, to set at liberty them that are bound; and then closing the book, said to the astonished multitude, This day is this Scripture fulfilled in your ears."

The time having arrived when he should assume the functions of his ministry, he was baptized in the river Jordan, by which rite he was solemnly initiated into those high offices which he was to fulfill as the Redeemer and Savior of the world.

Pursuing the history of St. Matthew, the next event following his baptism is the temptation. During forty days he permitted, and endured the assaults of Satan. And though his temptations were conducted with consummate art and skill, yet he was foiled in every onset, and the Savior was completely victorious. The views which this scene gives of the Redeemer's character, are in the highest degree instructive and salutary; while the issue of the conflict and the means of victory, furnish his disciples with weapons and encouragement under every assault of the prince of darkness.

Emerging from the wilderness, he came to Nazareth. Here his stay was brief. Thence he came and dwelt at Capernaum, a city on the north-west coast of the Sea of Tiberias. From this time the public ministry of Jesus began. Walking by the Sea of Galilee, "the shores of which," says Josephus, "are beautiful as Paradise," he saw and called his first disciples. Accompanied by them, he began his visits through Galilee, "teaching in their synagogues, and healing all manner of sickness and disease among the people." His preaching and miracles excited universal attention. His fame spread through all Syria, and vast numbers of people "followed him from Galilee, from Decapolis, from Jerusalem, and from beyond Jordan."

"And seeing the multitudes, he went up into a mountain." From an eminence he could more conveniently address the vast numbers who sought to hear and see him. A mountain is still shown, north-west of the ancient site of Capernaum, which tradition affirms to be the place where this sermon was delivered, and which is hence called the "Mount of Beatitudes." "And when he was set, his disciples came unto him." Sitting was the common attitude of Jewish teachers. "And he opened his mouth, and taught them." This is a mode of expression indicating the commencement of a solemn and lengthened discourse. Perhaps no where in the history of our blessed Savior have we a more interesting view of his character, as the great prophet of his Church, than in the scene now before us. The mountain, the preacher, the rapt multitude—every thing impresses; and then his discourse—every word comes sanctioned by Divine authority, and falls like a beam of light from the throne of God.

It would seem almost needless to remark, that religion was the subject of his teaching. He had come into the world to save men—to save them from ignorance, from guilt, and from the fearful penalties of sin in a future world. And all his teachings were designed to promote this benevolent result. Entering upon his public ministry, he began, at once, to declare the tidings of life and immortality. He preached salvation, and proclaimed the love of God to a perishing world. He announced the doctrines of religion, explained their nature, and enforced their necessity by the most awful sanctions. Religion had been obscured by the false glosses of men. In the hands of its professed teachers, it had sunk to a heartless observance of mere ceremony. The form was there, but the power had fled. It was a corpse decked in diamonds. To remove these false glosses, to restore to religion even more than primitive purity and power, and enthrone it in the heart, a living and sanctifying principle, was the great end and aim of the Savior. And never for a moment did he turn aside from this object. All his teachings centered here. Every remark, however casual or remote, in the beginning, at once took the direction, and finally rested upon the great question of our eternal interests. O how must that Savior have borne us upon his heart! how must he have loved us, when he could never speak, even, without revealing something of that deep interest which he felt in our welfare! Let us adore and love, with an ardent and supreme affection, that heavenly Teacher, whose character we are now to contemplate. And may a portion of that Spirit which rested on him without measure, fall on us, that we may "speak in demonstration of the Spirit and with power," upon this exalted theme! Your attention will be directed to a single leading thought—his characteristics as a teacher—and we can only speak of the more prominent.

I. He is a Divine Teacher.

He was commissioned by the Father, and in the fullness of time sent forth to make known the will of God, and the wondrous plan of redemption. Upon the divinity of his mission the Savior spoke often and fully. "I am come," says he, "in my Father's name. The living Father hath sent me. I came down from heaven, not to do mine own will, but the will of him that sent me. My meat is to do the will of him that sent me, and to finish his work." He was an embassador from heaven. His credentials bore the signature of the Almighty, under whose high authority he acted. But he is to be distinguished from all others in this capacity. Moses was a teacher; the prophets were teachers—they were divinely sent and divinely accredited; but they were not divine. He alone who "is in the bosom of the Father, full of grace and truth," could claim this distinction. He was the Son of God, and by this relationship could claim equality with the Father. "I and my Father are one. If ye had known me," said he to his disciples, "ye should have known my Father also; and from henceforth ye know him and have seen him." Could any man, or angel, utter such words? and do they not teach his supreme and absolute divinity? "In him," says an inspired apostle, "dwelt all the fullness of the Godhead bodily." And though he was the apostle of our profession, acting in the subordinate relation of a messenger to man, he was not the less equal with God; "being the brightness of the Father's glory, and the express image of his person."

The testimony of the Father still further confirms these views: "There is another that beareth witness of me: and I know that the witness which he witnesseth of me is true. The Father that sent me, he beareth witness of me." And that testimony was given in a manner fitted to impress us with the divinity of our Savior as the great prophet and teacher of righteousness. The first instance was at his baptism. As he was now about to enter upon his public ministry, it would seem important that some acknowledgment of his divine character and mission should be made. Testimony from heaven would give the greatest weight to his claims. Accordingly, when he ascended from the waters of Jordan, "the heavens were opened, and the Spirit of God, descending like a dove, lighted upon him; and lo, a voice from heaven, saying, This is my beloved Son, in whom I am well pleased."

Another was on the Mount of Transfiguration. "The object of this event," says Mr. Watson, "was probably the inauguration of Christ as the supreme Lawgiver and teacher of his Church." The scene was appropriate. Having ascended a mountain, attended by three of his disciples, "he was transfigured before them; and his face did shine as the sun, and his raiment was white as the light: and behold, there appeared unto them Moses and Elias talking with them. Then answered Peter, and said unto Jesus, Lord, it is good for us to be here." So you would have thought, and said, had you been there. "Let us make three tabernacles; one for thee, one for Moses, and one for Elias. While he yet spake, behold, a bright cloud overshadowed them: and behold, a voice out of the cloud, which said, This is my beloved Son, in whom I am well pleased: hear ye him." That voice attested not only his divinity, but his prophetic office likewise, and claimed for him supreme attention and implicit faith. The same voice speaks from Mount Tabor, which was heard amid the rolling clouds of smoke and flame at Sinai, and above the trumpet's waxing blast. "Hear ye him;" not Moses only, but that greater prophet of whom Moses spoke; not Elijah, or the prophets only, but him to whom they all gave witness. Hear ye him; at all times, on all occasions, on all subjects. Thus, in view of his divine character, are we required to take him for our only teacher—to sit at his feet, and learn of him the lessons of saving truth.

II. AUTHORITY WAS ANOTHER LEADING TRAIT IN HIS CHARACTER AS A TEACHER.

There was a seeming right to command, a weight and force of appeal that compelled his hearers to say, "Never man spake like this man." Nor was that authority merely seeming; it was not affected to gain attention—it was real—it was the voice of God. When, therefore, he taught on the Sabbath days, in Capernaum, we read, "they were astonished at his doctrine, for his word was with power."

His was the authority of infinite wisdom. "In him were hid all the treasures of wisdom and knowledge." He was the wisdom of God. Even his enemies, when they tauntingly said, "Is not this the carpenter's son?" were compelled to say, also, "Whence hath this man this wisdom and these mighty works?" That wisdom was displayed in all his discourses. When *he* taught, the truths of religion appeared in a new aspect. When he spoke of God, it was in language that showed his perfect knowledge of the divine nature and perfections. "No man," said he, "knoweth the Father, but the Son;"

and when he utters that sublime sentence, "God is a Spirit," we feel that the declaration is true. It was more than the combined wisdom of the world had ever said. He was acquainted with the entire condition of man. No one ever dissected the human heart as he did. His omniscient eye penetrated its most secret chambers, and showed us where to find the source of all those evils that have filled the world with crime and woe. "From within out of the heart of man proceed evil thoughts, adulteries, fornications, murders, thefts, covetousness, wickedness, deceit, lasciviousness, an evil eye, blasphemy, pride, foolishness." The experience of all ages has confirmed this wisdom. He was perfectly acquainted with the thoughts of men. He was never deceived by appearances—never made a false estimate of character. When many around him professed to receive his words and believe in him, he was not misled by their pretensions, because "he knew all men, and needed not that any should testify of man; for he knew what was in man."

Whatever might be the art or sagacity of his enemies, however wisely or secretly they might lay their schemes, he at once saw through their dissembling, and detected their wickedness. Take one instance of many: The Pharisees had counseled together how they might entangle him in conversation. Having arranged their plan, "they sent their disciples, saying, Master, we know that thou art true, and teachest the way of God in truth; neither carest thou for any man: for thou regardest not the person of men." This was a hypocritical compliment, not believed by them, but artfully said to conceal their designs.

"Tell us," said they, "is it lawful to give tribute to Cesar, or not?" But at once he perceived their object, and said, "Why tempt ye me, ye hypocrites? Show me the tribute money." And they brought him a penny. Then said he, "Whose image and superscription is this?" They replied, "Cesar's." Then said he, "Render unto Cesar the things which are Cesar's, and unto God the things that are God's." Thus were they foiled in their aim. His reply was so wise—it so clearly exposed their wickedness, that they went their way, utterly confounded and covered with shame.

His was the authority of infinite rectitude and purity. Even among men, with all their imperfections, personal rectitude gives authority to discourse. Thus the precepts of the virtuous have energy and force, while those of the vicious are empty and powerless. They fall short of the heart, because they lack the impulsive force of a holy life. The holiness of the Savior was perfect; it had neither mixture nor spot. In the language of St. Paul, "He was holy, harmless, and undefiled, separate and apart from sinners." No improper passion or desire dwelt in his bosom. He was unstained by crime and unspotted from the world. "He did no sin, neither was there guile in his mouth." When upon earth, and surrounded by perverse and censorious men, ever watchful as they were, they could find no fault in him. In all the majesty of conscious rectitude he could appeal to their own decision: "Which of you convinceth me of sin?"

His, too, was the authority of almighty power, exhibiting itself "in signs, and wonders, and mighty deeds," for the confirmation of his word. "The works that I do," said Jesus, "they bear witness of me." And what were these works? Let us take his own enumeration of them. "Go and tell John," said he, "the things which ye do see and hear. The blind receive their sight, the lame walk, the lepers are cleansed, the deaf hear, the dead are raised up, and the poor have the Gospel preached to them." Were such a teacher to address you, proclaiming himself the resurrection and the life, and then at once call from the grave a man that had been dead four days, who could question his power—who would not bow to his authority? Such a teacher we have in the person of Jesus Christ. The wide universe was under his control; every department of nature yielded to his sway; the winds and waves, every form of disease, angels in heaven, and men on earth confessed his authority; while the very demons of hell cried out for fear before him, and fled howling from his presence. The Jewish mind, dark and obdurate as it was, saw and felt the force of these proofs. "We know," said one of their wisest counselors, "that thou art a teacher come from God, for no man can do the works which thou doest except God be with him." Then, if infinite wisdom, infinite purity, and almighty power, exerting themselves for the alleviation of human sorrow, can confer authority, it is pre-eminently his, for he claimed and possessed them all. While contemplating his perfections, I feel that he has a right to speak, and bowing at his feet, I exclaim, "Speak, Lord, for thy servant heareth."

III. A THIRD CHARACTERISTIC OF HIS TEACHING WAS SIMPLICITY.

And in this there is a marked distinction between him and all other teachers. The heathen oracles taught; but they spoke in dark and mysterious words, and were far more likely to deceive than instruct. The Gentile philosophers drew around them disciples and taught, but they dealt in such subtile discourse and metaphysical reasoning, as to be little less obscure than the oracles of the groves and mountains. The rabbis among the Jews had their disciples and taught, but their glosses and fables so far dimmed the light of truth, that both they and their disciples alike remained in darkness. How striking was the contrast when the Savior taught! He not only revealed the truth, but explained it in such a sweet and familiar way as to leave the most ignorant without excuse. Those sublime and precious truths, so necessary for the world to know, were stripped of all obscurity and brought down to the most humble capacity. Even a child might know them and be made wise unto salvation. The attention of men, so difficult to arrest and hold, was at once secured by the most striking metaphors and beautiful parables, while by the same means the light of truth was carried into minds hitherto locked up in ignorance and sin. He had come into the world to teach men the way to heaven, and he stooped to every grade of mind, and every grade of condition, for the accomplishment of this benevolent end. He taught the humble fisherman by the seaside. In the field he instructs the husbandman how to sow, and how to cultivate the fruit of life eternal.

On the highway he finds the neglected beggar, and teaches him how to gain and keep the true riches. At the well, where he rested, faint and weary, he shows a despised Samaritan the way of salvation, and opens in her heart "a well of water springing up into everlasting life."

It would, perhaps, be impossible to bring forward a more striking example of simplicity, than is found in the sermon on the Mount. This is certainly one of the most lofty and sublime exhibitions of divine truth ever presented to the human mind; and yet such is its plainness that the most ordinary capacity can appreciate its beauty and feel its force. Look, for instance, at the manner in which he inculcates the doctrine of Divine providence, and the duty of confidence in its provisions: "Behold the fowls of the air: they sow not, neither do they reap, nor gather into barns; yet your heavenly Father feedeth them." How beautiful is this! When oppressed with desponding thoughts, we are to look at the birds. We see them flit on joyous wing; they sing in the groves, they meet the early dawn with songs, they pour their notes upon the evening gale, unanxious about the morrow. God feeds them. Will he not then supply your wants? Another illustration he takes from the lilies of the field: "See how they grow: they toil not, they spin not." Yet night and day they expand in beauty, spreading their blossoms to the sun and loading the air with perfume—"even Solomon was not arrayed in such glory!" Yet this beautiful flower will soon fade and be cut down. "And now," says Jesus, "if God thus clothes the lily, a frail flower, soon to perish, will he be unmindful of his children? Will he not much more clothe you?"

Look next at the manner in which he teaches prayer: "Ask, and it shall be given you; seek, and ye shall find; knock, and it shall be opened unto you. What man is there of you, whom if his son ask bread, will he give him a stone? or if he ask a fish, will he give him a serpent? If ye then being evil know how to give good gifts unto your children, how much more shall your Father which is in heaven give good things to them that ask him?" No one but the Son of God could teach such a lesson as this, at once so sublime and simple. A child can appreciate this illustration, and feel the sweet encouragement to pray. Henceforth the most dark and doubtful mind may look to heaven, with the glad assurance that God is far more ready to hear and answer the humble suppliant, than the most affectionate of earthly parents.

Looking into other discourses of our blessed Lord, we find every-where the same beautiful simplicity. "The common people heard him gladly." The illiterate multitude, so long despised by the proud scribe and Pharisee, hung upon his lips, charmed by his touching illustrations and the winning sweetness of his manner. The ignorant were no longer to perish for lack of knowledge, for infinite wisdom itself had come to be their instructor.

The teachings of Christ have, therefore, a universal fitness. They are adapted to all ages, all classes, all characters. They were designed for universal benefit, and ere he left the world he made ample arrangements for their diffusion among all nations.

The adaptation is complete, both to the wise and the unwise, the philosopher and the fool. And the blended grandeur and simplicity of his discourses, while they astonish the one, equally charm and delight the other. And still, the judgment and the sentiment of all who sit at his feet is, "Never man spake like this man."

IV. HE WAS AFFECTIONATE AND TENDER.

Something more is requisite in a teacher than authority and talent. Authority may awe, and great abilities may astonish; but neither of them soften and win the heart, unless tempered with gentleness and love. The Jewish doctors were proud and austere; there was nothing about them to attract and attach disciples; they repulsed rather than invited the ignorant and humble. How striking was the contrast when Jesus appeared! His heart was full of love. It was love that moved him to stoop from the throne of the universe and enter our dark world. It was love that impelled him onward in a career of unexampled benevolence, beset with suffering, persecution, and death; and all in our behalf. "Ye know the grace of our Lord Jesus Christ, who, though he was rich, yet for our sakes became poor, that we, through his poverty, might be rich." Yes, it was infinite love; nothing less could suggest the idea of such condescension, or propose such a sublime result. And that love shone brighter than the sun in all that he uttered, and in all that he did, while he dwelt in our world. None ever had such a heart as Jesus. It was appropriately the home of love, or, more properly, it was the inexhaustible fountain from whence all love proceeds. It bore him through the sorrows of the garden and the cross; and now that he has returned to his native heaven, he is still the same. Though on yonder throne of glory,

> "His heart is made of tenderness,
> His bowels melt with love."

His subjects of discourse indicate the feelings of his heart. Man is a moral being, and bound to an immortal destiny. He is also a fallen being; an original taint affects his nature. "The whole head is sick, the whole heart is faint." His life is one of rebellion against God, made up of daily transgressions. He is an alien from the family of God, cut off from its privileges, and the heir of future and endless wrath. But may he be pardoned? may he regain what he has lost? may he ever return to the pure and peaceful family of God? If so, how? How intensely interesting are these questions! their very utterance sends a thrill to the inmost soul! A teacher who would devote his life to these questions, who would resolve our doubts, and strike out the path of return, might well be regarded as the friend of man; and if he should close his labor of love by dying, that we might live forever, the proof of his affection would be complete.

This is precisely what the Savior has done; forever blessed be his name! He came to the world with a message of mercy, and his entire life was consecrated to the one work of making known the way of salvation. For what purpose he came—how great was our guilt and danger—how God loved us—how we might escape the wrath to come—how we might be pardoned and purified—how we might regain more than Paradise, these were his only themes of discourse. For this every occasion was improved and every moment occupied. Immortal souls were perishing, and moments were too precious to be wasted. Passing from the temple on one occasion, "the disciples saw a blind man; and they said, Master, who did sin, this man, or his parents, that he was born blind?" It was probably Sabbath evening; the sun was sinking in the western sky, and the shades of night about to appear. Turning to them, he uttered these impressive words, "I must work the works of him that sent me while it is day: the night cometh when no man can work;" and then, by an exertion of infinite power, restored the blind to sight. This was the diligence of love, exerting its energies every moment in bearing away the sins and sorrows of mankind.

Look at his manner of teaching. "Learn of me," said he, "for I am meek and lowly in heart." This is intended to express the gentleness and kindness of his manner toward those who place themselves under his instructions. As if he had said, "You need not fear, I will deal tenderly with you, and bear with all your infirmities; you may be sinful, but I came to save sinners; you may be ignorant, but I will not cast out any that come to me. 'The bruised reed will I not break, and the smoking flax will I not quench.'" In all this, how beautifully does his love appear! Were it otherwise, conscious of his many defects, the sinner would fear to approach him, and shrink with trembling from his presence; but, with a heart full of love, and a face beaming with kindness, he says, "Come." And when, in obedience to his invitation, we sit down at his feet, he graciously condescends to our ignorance. Are we slow to learn? he does not chide, but repeats his lessons, giving line upon line, and precept upon precept. When we fail, he does not frown us from his presence, but gently prompts us to try again; and thus he advances as we can bear it, till the bright rays of truth light up the whole mind, and the soul quickens into a new and heavenly life.

Observe his invitations and offers. "Come," said he, "unto me, all ye that labor and are heavy laden, and I will give you rest." If more than this is wanting, take his declaration in the synagogue of Nazareth: "The Spirit of the Lord is upon me, because he hath anointed me to preach the Gospel to the poor; he hath sent me to heal the broken-hearted, to preach deliverance to the captives, and recovering of sight to the blind; to set at liberty them that are bound." Draw near now, and lay open your complaints. Are you poor? the "poor have the Gospel preached unto them;" and if you will receive the message, it will enrich and bless you forever. Are you broken-hearted? "he is nigh unto them that are of a broken heart, and saveth such as be of a contrite spirit." Are you enslaved? he comes proclaiming deliverance to the captives; and not this alone, but he shall open the doors of your prison house, break off your fetters, and "set at liberty them that are bound." What offers are these! How full of grace and love! They should relieve every difficulty, suppress every fear, and banish doubt forever from the mind.

And look, too, at his grief under the perversity

and opposition of men. Standing in the midst of a world of dying sinners, his gracious announcement was, "I am come, that ye might have life, and that ye might have it more abundantly." And when they rejected his merciful offers, he exclaimed, in pity and sorrow, "Ye will not come unto me, that ye might have life."

One of the most touching scenes, illustrative of these generous feelings, occurred near the period of his sufferings. He was about to enter Jerusalem. As he approached it he passed over the Mount of Olives. From that mountain there was a full view of the city. The view of the splendid capital, the knowledge of its crimes, its guilt, and the storm of vengeance that was about to burst upon it, filled his bosom with unutterable pity; "and he wept over it, saying, If thou hadst known, even thou in this thy day, the things which belong unto thy peace; but now they are hid from thine eyes." What a lesson for ministers!

> "Did Christ o'er sinners weep;
> And shall our cheeks be dry?"

No, we too should weep. The love of Christ is as deep now as then; the soul is as precious, the danger of sinners as imminent. Pity becomes the servant of a weeping Savior. If compelled to utter the sentence of death, like Jesus on Olivet, let us bathe it with our tears.

V. FINALLY, IT WAS CHARACTERISTIC OF HIM AS A TEACHER, THAT ALL HIS INSTRUCTIONS WERE EMBODIED IN HIS OWN BLESSED EXAMPLE.

Nothing is more important in a religious teacher than this. We may have wisdom, eloquence, and authority; but *example* is the *great* teacher. Hence, our Savior embodied his doctrines in his life. From him we not only have the sublimest lessons, but we see them exemplified—invested with a body, living and moving before the world. Let us select a few instances.

He taught the duty of humility; and his life was the pattern. Though he was Lord of the universe, and "equal with God, yet he made himself of no reputation, and took upon him the form of a servant." He served men, even his enemies, the poorest and the vilest of mankind. He condescended to the lowest offices—washing his disciples' feet. He was not emulous of distinction, but rejected the praise of men, and cast aside the honors of the world; and, finally, descending to a point beyond which humility itself could not go, "he became obedient unto death, even the death of the cross."

He taught meekness; and he excelled all men in this grace. Under the greatest provocations, when reproached and vilified, when classed with the lowest and vilest of men, he was tranquil and self-possessed. No breath of calumny or storm of persecution could agitate his placid heart. He never displayed unholy passion, or evinced a spirit of resentment. "When he was reviled, he reviled not again." He wept over his enemies, and, when suffering all that their malice could inflict, prayed that the men who nailed him to the tree might be forgiven.

He taught obedience to God; and his life was in harmony with the Divine will. "My meat," said he, "is to do the will of him that sent me, and to finish his work." Every desire, and purpose, and thought, was in beautiful and perfect agreement with the spotless mind of God.

He inculcated a pure and fervent devotion; and it distinguished his life. He held constant communion with God, and in the sacred exercise of prayer spent even whole nights. Whether we see him in the synagogue or in the temple, on the Mount with his disciples or at the grave of Lazarus, his friend, in the garden or on the cross, he is still a man of prayer. Prayer was the element in which he lived and died.

He taught the doctrine of Christian benevolence; and his life exemplified it. Love drew him from the skies, and is the true principle upon which to account for the wonders of his life and death. He gave himself a ransom for sinful men, and by this, together with a life of unexampled benevolence, brought before the world a display and a manner of love that passeth understanding. "*Herein* is love, not that we loved God, but that *he* loved us." Here, then, is both our teacher and our pattern. But O, Jesus of Nazareth, what a character is thine! "Thou art fairer than the children of men: grace is poured into thy lips; therefore, thou art blessed forever." How precious are thy words, how perfect is thine example, my teacher, my pattern! As such I receive thee, to hear thy words and imitate thy life.

Conclusion.

I shall close these considerations with a single inference: *If Christ is a divine teacher, we should hear him.* Hark! "A voice from the most excellent glory" proclaims, "This is my beloved Son: hear ye him." A divine command makes it our duty; and "to-day, if ye will hear his voice, harden not your hearts." Hear him in his word. Search the Scriptures; they are able to make you wise unto salvation. Hear him in his house; he speaks through his embassadors, who "beseech you in Christ's stead to be reconciled to God."

Do I address one who refuses to listen to the voice of this heavenly Teacher? Your condition is most alarming. It is one of sin and guilt; nay, more, if more is possible—it is one of danger—danger of death eternal—a danger you can *never* escape if you continue in sin. The soul that sinneth shall *die*. "Except ye repent," says the Son of God, "ye shall all likewise perish." There is hope for you, but that hope rests upon your repentance. If you will come to him, if you will hear his voice, you shall find salvation; but if not, then you *must* perish; no arm in the universe can save you. "See, then, that ye refuse not him that speaketh; for if they escaped not who refused him that spake on earth, much more shall not we escape, if we turn away from him that speaketh from heaven."

Perhaps I speak to one who is saying, "Jesus, thou Son of David, have mercy upon me!" Rise, he calleth thee. "Come unto me all ye that labor and are heavy laden, and I will give you rest." Ah! that is the same sweet voice that was heard among the hills and vales of Judea, eighteen hundred years ago; it is still a voice of love. "Blessed are the people that know the joyful sound." Come, then, and bow at his feet. He will not frown thee thence, for he casteth out none that come to him.

Believe his word. Trust his grace. Cast thyself upon his mercy. Then thou shalt find that "his words are spirit and life." He will take away thy load of guilt; he will heal thy wounded soul, and pour such heavenly light upon thee, that thy heart shall bound for joy, and thy tongue shall sing for gladness.

Do I address any of his disciples? Yes. Like Matthew you were pursuing the world, but Jesus said to you, "Follow me;" and you arose and followed him. "Verily, I say unto you, there is no man that hath left houses, or brethren, or sisters, or father, or mother, or wife, or children, or lands for my sake and the Gospel's, but shall receive an hundred-fold, now in this time, and in the world to come eternal life." Cleave to him. Your true position is at his feet, drinking in his precious words. "You know the truth, and the truth hath made you free." Let none seduce you from his cause. He has now gone to his throne. Take up your cross and follow him to heaven. Some, deceived by Satan, and insnared by the world, have turned aside. "Will ye *also* go away? Lord, to *whom* should we go but to *thee?* *Thou* hast the words of eternal life."

LECTURE II.

FIRST BEATITUDE.

"Blessed are the poor in spirit: for theirs is the kingdom of heaven." MATTHEW v, 3.

"THE Old Testament," says one of the old divines, "closes with a curse, but the New opens with a blessing." Christ, therefore, begins his sermon on the Mount with blessings; as if he intended, at this early period of his ministry, to intimate the merciful design of his mission: that "he came into the world not to condemn the world, but that the world through him might be saved;" and that, opening his mission in this way, he meant to go on, adding blessing to blessing, till the subjects of his grace should be completely and eternally happy.

These eight beatitudes may be regarded as so many moral portraits; and nothing could more certainly arrest the mind and fix the attention of men, than the characters thus represented, and the blessings pronounced upon them. Heretofore men had looked upon them in a far different light. When had the poor in spirit, or the mourner, or the meek, been pronounced happy? Never. They had been universally regarded as mean and despicable. "There was not," says Mr. Wesley, "in the whole Roman language, with all the improvements of the Augustan age, so much as a name for humility; nor was one found in all the copious language of Greece, till it was made by the great apostle." This, then, was a new doctrine, contrary to the most cherished views of the human heart, calculated, perhaps, to rouse prejudice and opposition—certainly to fill the mind with wonder. The multitudes that heard him were astonished at his doctrine.

Perhaps one leading design of the Savior in these beatitudes, was to rectify our views upon the subject of happiness. Happiness is what all men everywhere pursue; and "who will show us any good?" is a universal inquiry. Man can not desire misery—he *must* desire happiness. A law of his nature compels it. The desire was implanted by an all-wise Creator, and for the most benevolent ends. But in what does it consist, and where shall it be found? Alas! in regard to nothing has a blind and erring world made so many mistakes! Some pursue it in courts and palaces, others in literary distinction. Some, again, in the acquisition of wealth, and others in sensual pleasure. But in all these and a thousand other cases happiness is a flying phantom, that eludes the pursuit and mocks the hopes of men. "The deep saith, It is not in me; and the sea saith, It is not with me: it can not be gotten for gold, neither shall silver be weighed for the price thereof." The objects usually sought by men, as wealth, honor, and influence, can not confer happiness; they have no adaptation to this end, and all who have sought it in them, have, sooner or later, realized the bitterness of disappointment. Millions are thus insnared and cheated. Happiness, like a bright vision, floats far away before them. Eager in the pursuit, "they take no note of time," but traverse the whole path of life, and finally drop into the grave ruined and wretched forever. O, might we learn wisdom from their folly!

And now, would we learn what happiness is, and where it is to be found, we must take our first lessons of Jesus; we must learn of him, for he alone can show us the way of life. Let us, then, with Mary sit down at his feet. This itself will be the first step in the path of bliss—a path growing brighter in its progress till it terminates in the perfect bliss of the kingdom of God. His first lesson is, "Blessed are the poor in spirit: for theirs is the kingdom of heaven." Let us now

I. Institute this very plain question: Who are the poor in spirit?

This inquiry is both important and necessary. To gain the promised boon we must be such. The investigation is, therefore, most essential. To prevent mistake, I remark, in the first place, they are not the poor in worldly estates—the destitute, in opposition to those who possess the plenty of wealth. The poor are not always virtuous and happy. Often life is imbittered to them by the stings of remorse, as well as by the distresses of poverty. Many of them, after a life of toil and want, enter upon the future world with only the prospect of endless sorrow.

They are not the patient and contented poor. Many seem content with poverty who can lay no claim to religion. They are satisfied with their condition from the mere love of indolence. Our Savior is not here teaching the value of contentment, but laying the foundation of a holy life—a structure of such magnitude as to require a firmer support than mere contentment with our lot. And besides, true contentment is a fruit of religion, not its foundation.

Nor is it the love of poverty. This may exist where true poverty of spirit is unknown. It may spring from mere caprice, disgust with the world, or mistaken views of duty. Men have sometimes renounced the world, have clothed themselves in sackcloth, and in caves and deserts have endured all the wants and woes of poverty; consoling themselves, meanwhile, that they were the heirs of the promised kingdom of God; but it is not upon such the Savior looks when he confers this blessing. No; these are mistaken views, false principles of action, which always stunt the growth of piety and contract the sphere of Christian usefulness. To all such I would say, go out into the world. Let your light shine before men—do good. The wide field of Christian effort is before you—toil there; and then, indeed, will you inherit the full blessedness both of the present and future kingdom of God.

Nor are the spiritually poor intended. This is not only an unfortunate but a sinful estate. It is to be destitute of grace and goodness, "without God and without hope in the world." These are the subjects of present guilt and future wrath. The promised bliss of the kingdom of God pertains not to them.

By the poor in spirit the Savior means the truly humble. In this way they are often distinguished. "Thus saith the high and lofty One that inhabiteth eternity, My name is holy; I dwell in the high and holy place, with him also that is of an humble and a contrite heart. To this man will I look, even to him that is poor and of a contrite heart, and that trembleth at my word." When the disciples of Jesus strove for pre-eminence and disputed for the chief place in his kingdom, he taught them by a symbol the most beautiful and impressive, that humility was the grand prerequisite to the honors he had to bestow. "Calling a little child, he set him in the midst and said, Except ye be converted and become as little children, ye can not enter the kingdom of heaven." Here, then, the poor, the contrite of heart, and the humble are all the same, and their appropriate emblem is the unaffected humility of a little child.

While we are enabled by these views to determine the character the Savior intends, we perceive, also, the importance of humility, and the relation it bears to the entire Christian character. It is the starting-point in the religion of a sinner—it associates itself with every duty—it is present in all his joys—it distinguishes his profession of Christ before the world—it abounds in all the deportment of life, till finally it becomes the habit of the soul, and he is "*clothed* with humility."

1. *Poverty of spirit stands in direct opposition to the native pride of the human heart.*

Pride was an ingredient in the first transgression, and has since become a characteristic sin of man. It reigns in every bosom, and spreads through every department of society. Self-praise and self-sufficiency, personal adornment, envy, desire of applause, impatience, and rebellion against God are among the ordinary developments of this hateful spirit. Seated in the soul and wrapped in the robes of its own importance, it never speaks but in terms of self-applause. "I am rich and increased in goods;" "I sit a queen, and shall see no sorrow," is its deceptive and lying strain. Alas, to what a mortifying reverse shall the proud of heart be subjected—stripped of their shining robes, thrust down to perdition, and covered with "everlasting shame and contempt!"

Pride is a kind of parent sin, and prolific of evil. It stands related to almost every form of wickedness that blots the character of individual and social life. Hence springs impenitence and contempt of divine mercy. "The wicked through the pride of his countenance will not seek after God." Why should he? He has no realizing sense of his guilt and sin, or his need of mercy. These are the men of whom the Psalmist says, "Pride compasseth them as a chain, violence covereth them as a garment; therefore, they set their mouth against the heavens, and their tongue walketh through the earth." Is it wonderful that God abhors this daring arrogance, and that he will strike it down from its airy hights—down to the lowest hell?

Poverty of spirit is the reverse of this. As pride exalts the soul, humility abases it. As pride inspires it with ideas of its own importance, humility disperses such false conceits, and uncovers its utter poverty and helplessness. Here religion begins in deep self-abasement before God. It can begin no where else. As long as pride exalts the soul, filling it with opinions of its own worth and consequence, religion can not enter; the soul remains in the "gall of bitterness and in the bond of iniquity."

Pride counteracts every spiritual and saving influence. Just views of God, of Christ, of our condition and relations, are impossible while it rules the heart. All views upon these subjects are distorted, because seen through a false medium and from a false position. Under these circumstances we can not appreciate the character of Christ as a Savior; we do not feel our sinfulness; we do not feel the necessity of an interest in the Redeemer's blood; nor can we till willing to know the plague of our hearts, and take our true position in the estimation of God and man.

2. *A sense of utter destitution forms an obvious trait in the character of the poor in spirit.*

As temporal poverty implies the want of what is necessary for the body, so spiritual poverty implies the want of what is necessary for the soul. No poverty is so deplorable as that which sin has introduced. It has robbed us of every good, and despoiled the heart of its richest treasures. The conviction of this is not easily fixed in the soul; and hence, many, like a fallen Church of old, are saying, "I am rich and increased in goods, and have need of nothing." Sad and ruinous mistake! Alas, how blinding is the influence of sin! How strange a delusion to judge the most abject poverty affluence; and to fancy the very pangs of distress tokens of prosperity! Such mistakes men are making every day. Every sinner is acting under this delusion, and, therefore, refuses to humble himself before God, and spurns from him the offers of divine mercy. But the poor in spirit are acquainted with their condition. The Spirit of God has convinced them of sin, and they now see that they are "wretched, and poor, and blind, and naked." Like the ruined prodigal they have come to themselves. The delusion is at an end, and they awake to find themselves far from home, in a degrading bondage, and in utter destitution.

Thus enlightened, they perceive that they are destitute of all good. Not more keenly do the homeless poor, bereft of every earthly comfort, feel their misery, than those whose hearts have been led to realize their lost condition by sin. It was under such humiliating views as these that Paul exclaimed, "I know that in me, that is, in my flesh, dwelleth no good thing." Spiritual good, the original wealth of man, has been utterly wasted and spent in sin. Like Naomi, they went into a land of strangers full, but they have returned empty. Even the nakedness of Egypt, when stripped by utter famine, can not fitly represent their impoverished state. Of themselves they have no good thing; no strength or wisdom; no goodness of heart or life. The self-righteousness in which they trusted has vanished like an unreal vision, and left them without a plea and without a hope. Instead of the good heart of which they boasted, they see it as wholly sinful and wholly corrupt. Instead of the faultless life, so long regarded with complacency, they now behold naught but "filthy rags," the affecting proofs of their alienation from God. Boasting ends, and, covered with shame and confusion of face, they sink down in the very dust before God. I have been led to take these views from that impressive statement of St. Paul's, in the second chapter of Ephesians. To fix our attention and lead us to humility, he says, "Where fore, *remember* that at that time ye were without Christ, being aliens from the commonwealth of Israel, and strangers from the covenants of promise, having no hope, and without God in the world." Such is the state of man by nature; a state so humiliating, that the bare remembrance of it should banish pride and self-confidence forever from the heart. It is the vivid impression of this that produces poverty of spirit, and sinks the soul in deep abasement before God.

3. *Poverty of spirit implies, not only the absence of good, but the presence of evil.*

There is the evil of sin. The poor in spirit have a felt experience of this. A beggar upon his pallet of straw, amid the darkness of night, may fancy himself in a palace surrounded with all the splendor of wealth. But when the sun arises and shines upon him, the dream dissolves, and all the evils of poverty stare him in the face. So, when the Spirit shines upon the dark heart, its true character and state are seen. He is now "convinced of sin, of righteousness, and of judgment to come." The follies of childhood, the misdeeds of youth, and the iniquities of riper years are seen. The sins of his heart, and lips, and hands, are seen—his sins at home and abroad; in company and alone; in business and pleasure, are seen. His vanity and pride, his impatience and rebellion, his broken vows and stifled convictions, his abuse of God's mercy and rejection of his dear Son—these, too, he sees, so many and so great they can not be numbered. Who can tell how oft he has sinned? We can reckon our pulses as they beat; we can number the moments as they fly; but who can compute the number of his iniquities?

And furthermore, in the language of Mr. Wesley, "his guilt is now before his face; he knows the punishment he has incurred, were it only on account of the corruption of his nature; how much more on account of his evil desires and thoughts, of his simple words and actions! He can not doubt for a moment, but the least of these deserves the damnation of hell, 'the worm that dieth not, and the fire that shall never be quenched.' Above all, the guilt of not believing on the only-begotten Son of God lies heavy upon him. He that believeth not is condemned already, and the wrath of God abideth on him."

4. *Another distinguishing trait in the character before us, is his sense of helplessness.*

Conscious of his exceeding sinfulness, and his exposure to future wrath, he feels that he can do nothing to extricate himself from the perils of his condition. Of himself he has no hope and no plea, and utterly despairing, he exclaims: "Who shall deliver me from this body of death?" Nor are these views erroneous—the result of excited fears or a disordered fancy; they are the effects of divine illumination, and harmonize with the real condition of man. For a man to begin religion upon the supposition of his own ability or worthiness, is to build without a foundation, or, at best, to build upon a deceitful quicksand, which will finally sink and ingulf him in hopeless ruin. It is to start for heaven upon a falsehood, which, however plausible it may now seem, will, sooner or later, display its true character, and end in the bitterness of disappointment.

We can render no satisfaction for past sins. The law of God demands perfect obedience. We have failed to render it, and are therefore accursed. Now, how shall we escape the awful penalty of the violated law? "Will the Lord be pleased with thousands of burnt-offerings, or with thousands of rivers of oil? Shall I give my first-born for my transgressions, the first of my body for the sin of my soul?" No; these can never take away sin. Will repentance avail? No; repentance is the acknowledgment of guilt, and the desert of punishment; not a reason for pardon. Will future obedience avail? This may meet future claims, but can never cancel past obligations, or form a reason why past offenses should be forgiven. We are left, then, under the full weight and burden of the curse—a curse that must pursue and burn against us forever. And not only are we without merit, but without strength. A moral weakness has come upon us, which cuts off every prospect of deliverance, and shuts us up to all the horrors of a sinful and ruined condition. Such views are fitted still further to humble the awakened sinner, to convince him of his unworthiness, to strip him of all self-dependence, and lead him to trust in the merits of the Son of God. Such is precisely the experience of the poor in spirit. Humiliation, self-distrust, and self-loathing are the marks that distinguish this character—marks that attract the notice of angels, and call forth the compassion of Jesus. Yes, he feels his sin and guilt, his want and helplessness. And this feeling is no slight and superficial thing, but one of terrible reality and depth. His heart is overwhelmed with a sense of utter desolation and inevitable ruin. He sinks in the dust, and, like the terror-stricken jailer, exclaims, "What *must* I do to be saved?" Now he prays. And nothing is more befitting his condition than prayer; for prayer is the cry of conscious want and misery. Look at the starving beggar; when he asks you for bread, his soul is in his words. You refuse, but this does not silence him. He asks again and again, till his prayer has touched your heart. Why? Because he is perishing. He must have bread or die. So prays the poor in spirit. It is the prayer of earnestness and feeling, inspired and sustained by the Holy Spirit; and, though seeming delays may distress, they neither silence his prayer nor abate his earnestness. He feels himself perishing, and, heedless of derision and scorn, lies pleading in the dust, as when a man doomed to death pleadeth for his life.

5. *The poor in spirit are distinguished by their entire dependence upon Christ.*

Poverty is always dependent, and lives upon the benefactions of others. The nature of the case as well as the beautiful promise of the Savior, given to the humble, requires of them an implicit trust in the Redeemer of the world. This is the great condition of receiving the kingdom of God; and every thing in their previous experience is preparatory to this. The dethronement of pride; the humiliation of the heart; the felt absence of good and presence of evil, with the sense of helpless misery, that afflicts them, all precede and prepare the way for that act of humble trust in Christ which secures to the soul an interest in the riches of redeeming mercy.

As an object of trust the atonement forms the only sure ground of hope to a perishing sinner. "Other foundation can no man lay." Christ, and Christ alone; the Lamb slain for sinners; his availing blood; his infinite merit; his all-sufficient righteousness—these constitute the only foundation; and a safe one—one that shall abide the changes of human opinion—the revolutions of time and the shock of dissolving worlds. Thank God, amid this ever-shifting scene, "here is firm footing, here is solid rock," "and he that believeth upon Him shall not be ashamed." Upon Him the truly humble depend. Though in himself nothing—all weakness, all poverty, yet he beholds in the adorable Redeemer an infinite wealth and fullness; not like a concealed spring, or fountain shut up, but like a wide, expansive ocean, free and open for all. In himself no being in the universe is poorer, but reposing in Christ, no being in the universe is richer. He has all things in Christ. "A man in one of the eastern cities had failed for a large amount. His credit was gone; his family in poverty, and himself involved in heavy liabilities. He surrendered his whole estate, and stood worse than penniless before the world. He had a brother, however, in the city, who possessed vast wealth. From him he received a power of attorney to transact business in his name. On his authority, and through the influence of his name, he at once commenced business as an efficient and prosperous merchant. 'In myself,' said this man to a friend, 'I have no credit; no man will trust me with a single bale of goods; yet I am really worth all my brother is worth. I sometimes offer to purchase of an individual on my own credit. He will not trust me a farthing. I tell him I wish to purchase on my brother's account. I can then buy every article in his store.'" And thus, whatever may be their poverty, the humble have infinite treasures in Jesus Christ. Faith makes them theirs. Their prayer for help is heard. God bows down his ear and listens to their requests. He opens the stores of grace, and bids them ask what they will. The response is:

"A guilty, weak, and helpless worm,
Into thine arms I fall;
Be *thou* my strength and righteousness—
My Jesus and my all."

And here we may begin to perceive the blessedness of this character. As intense glooms precede the breaking day, so the humility, the increasing sense of want and helplessness of the poor in spirit, indicate approaching relief and the light and joy of a full deliverance. "Blessed," says Jesus, "are the poor in spirit, for theirs is the kingdom of heaven." Let us then turn from the characters themselves, to reflect,

II. On the dignities and privileges to which they are raised.

Theirs is the kingdom of heaven. There is here a point of difference in relation to the kingdoms of this world and the kingdom of Christ which we should not overlook. If we seek the heirs of the former, we go to the palaces of the noble and the courts of kings. They are distinguished by their lofty bearing, and by the splendor of their equipage—by a ribbon or star denoting elevated rank. Would we find the heirs of the latter, we must descend into the vale of humility, where the Son of God once dwelt, and where dwell the lowly and the contrite of heart. These are they who shall wear crowns of life, and sit on thrones in heaven, and participate in the royal triumphs of the Son of God.

The phrases, "kingdom of heaven," and "kingdom of God," are often used in the New Testament. Their meaning is the same. They comprehend two leading ideas: Grace here, and glory hereafter; the enjoyment of spiritual religion in the present life, and the everlasting fruition of God in the life to come. To the first of these our Savior alludes when he says: "Behold, the kingdom of God is within you;" and to the second, when he declares, "that many shall come from the east and from the west, and shall sit down with Abraham, and Isaac, and Jacob in the kingdom of heaven."

1. *The kingdom of heaven, as a present and gracious estate, is theirs.*

It is set up in their hearts. God himself sits enthroned in the affections, and subduing every adverse principle, and bringing into captivity every thought to the obedience of Christ, reigns supreme, the adored Lord and Lawgiver of the soul.

The precise nature of this kingdom is beautifully described by St. Paul: "It is not meat and drink, but righteous peace and joy in the Holy Ghost." This is a most important statement, and shows us that religion consists, not in empty forms, but in a right state of heart, in spiritual and holy affections. This, however, is not a righteousness derived from the law, the result of obedience to its precepts.

This is impossible; "for all have sinned." It is the "righteousness of faith," or, "faith counted to us for righteousness;" so that we are accepted of God, not because we have never sinned, but because we have believed in Jesus. "Not to him that worketh, but to him that believeth on him that justifieth the ungodly, his faith is counted for righteousness." This kingdom, then, is "righteousness;" the justification of the soul before God; the knowledge of salvation by the remission of sins; a consciousness of pardon; "a divine persuasion wrought in the soul that Christ hath loved me and given himself for me." He "who has fled for refuge to the hope set before him," *knows* this. He has the joyful evidence in his own bosom, that "his sins are blotted out, and his iniquities carried away into a land of forgetfulness." "What," says Mr. Wesley, "is righteousness, but the life of God in the soul; the image of God stamped upon the heart, now renewed after the likeness of him that created it? What is it but the love of God, because he first loved us, and the love of all mankind for his sake?"

Another element in his kingdom is "peace;" peace with God; a sweet serenity of mind, arising from reconciliation with God. Enmity is now changed to love, and variance to friendship. The sweet light of peace irradiates the soul and reigns within, even while storms and tempests rage without. "The peace of God which passeth understanding, now keeps the heart and mind through Christ Jesus." The conscience, too, is pacified, and the mind is tranquil as a summer sea. They have peace with men. This is ever the result of receiving the kingdom of God. It puts an end to strife and bitterness, and produces concord and love. Whenever the heart is brought under the influence of this kingdom, enmity expires and universal love to man prevails. "Charity, that suffereth long and is kind, that beareth all things and endureth all things," is now put on as the apparel of the soul and the "bond of perfectness."

"And joy in the Holy Ghost." Religion has to do with the feelings as well as the intellect. When this heavenly kingdom is set up in the heart it is happy. However it may have been bowed down before, it now swells with inexpressible joy. The sun of glory has now risen upon the poor in spirit, and they rejoice in God through our Lord Jesus Christ. A most touching and beautiful illustration of this is found in Taylor's Life of Cowper. For a long time that gifted poet was oppressed with a dreadful melancholy, which was finally hightened to despair. Here he was found and delivered by the Friend of sinners. Speaking of his conversion, and the effects it produced upon him, he says: "Unless the arms of the Almighty had been under me, I should have been overwhelmed with gratitude and joy. My eyes filled with tears, and my voice choked with transport. I could only look up to heaven with silent awe, filled with love and wonder. How glad was I now to spend every moment in prayer and thanksgiving! I lost no opportunity of repairing to a throne of grace; but flew to it with an earnestness irresistible, and never to be satisfied." "*Blessed* are the poor in spirit!" Were there no higher honors, and no kingdom yet to be revealed, this is enough to insure their bliss. God of my fathers, number *me* with them. Be mine their humility and their blessedness; for he whom *thou* blessest is blessed indeed.

2. *Theirs, too, is the kingdom of heaven, as a future and glorious inheritance.*

There is such an inheritance. Beyond this stormy scene there is a pure and happy world. It is distinguished in the Bible as "the kingdom of God—the everlasting kingdom of our Lord Jesus Christ, an inheritance incorruptible, undefiled, and that fadeth not away." The throne of God and the Lamb are there. It is a kingdom of holiness and love; and happiness, like a broad and smiling sky, overspreads and surrounds all the inhabitants of that blessed world. Many are there; among them I see the holy Enoch; Moses, the man of God, and the long line of prophets gathered home before the coming of Christ, are there. John the Baptist is there. There are the apostles and precious early Christians. The reformers of the dark age are there. The pious of the last generation, and the first-fruits of the present day—all are there, each one walking in white, for they are worthy. This is the kingdom bestowed upon the poor in spirit, so bestowed that it is *now* theirs.

It is theirs by virtue of their relation to God. Having been brought into the kingdom of grace, they are now the children of God. We have seen the grandeur of their estate; let us look at the solidity of their title. It is displayed by St. Paul. His argument is short, but firm: "If children, then heirs"—no conclusion can be more just—"heirs of God and joint-heirs with Christ." And as they are now one with Christ, they shall share in his everlasting kingdom.

It is theirs by promise. Let the mind dwell on one promise of the Savior: "Let not your heart be troubled: ye believe in God, believe also in me. In my Father's house are many mansions; if it were not so, I would have told you. I go to prepare a place for you. And if I go and prepare a place for you, I will come again and receive you to myself; that where I am there ye may be also." This is enough.

It is theirs by anticipation and foretaste. "They look for a city which hath foundations, whose builder and maker is God." And how blessed is this hope! It enlightens in darkness; it strengthens in weakness; it supports in trial; it comforts in sorrow. Meanwhile, they enjoy the foretastes of that kingdom. As the subjects of grace, they have the beginning of glory. These kingdoms are one, differing only in maturity and perfection. This below leads to that above, and he who has entered the one has a joyful earnest of the other. "I am," says St. Peter, "a partaker of the glory that shall be revealed." This was not only *his* experience, but in the case of *every* believer that glory admits of a present participation. Each can sing,

"O what a blessed hope is ours!
While here on earth we stay,
We more than taste the heavenly powers,
And antedate that day."

Such is the import of this beautiful promise, and such the present bliss and future honors of the poor in spirit. The full possession will soon be given.

And as we see them there arrayed in the white garments of heaven, having crowns on their heads, and palms in their hands, we involuntarily exclaim, "*Blessed are the poor in spirit, for theirs is the kingdom of heaven!*"

CONCLUSION.

The one great truth we are to learn from this subject is, *The real value of humility.* Comparatively few estimate it according to its real value. Many treat it with contempt, and pour derision upon the lowly and humble of mind. This is the world's judgment. But what is God's? It is this: "Every one that humbleth himself shall be exalted." He places it foremost in the list of virtues, and will set it highest upon the thrones of heaven. He has declared that he will "resist the proud," and thrust them down to hell, but that he will exalt the poor in spirit to his presence, where they shall outshine the angels and be like the Son of God.

I see then what I ought most of all to desire and seek; not wealth, not worldly distinction, but humility. This, by God's help, shall be my aim. This shall be my perfection, to possess the mind which was also in Christ Jesus my Lord. I will regard every thing an evil that hinders this attainment, and every thing a good that secures its possession. It shall be my wealth in poverty, my joy in sorrow, and its promised rewards shall cheer me in all trials, and sustain me in all sufferings.

O, wouldst thou enjoy the kingdom of God? Humble thyself under his mighty hand. O man, thou art a sinner, poor and blind, and miserable and naked! Thou hast no hope, no plea—utterly condemned and utterly helpless. *Feel* this and bow down thy head in the dust. Let thy prayer, like the afflicted woman, be, "Lord, help me!" Or, like the storm-tossed disciples, "Lord, save or I perish." Look to the mighty Savior, and cast thy soul on him.

"None but Jesus, none but Jesus
Can do helpless sinners good."

And his promises, O hear them, and believe. "For he shall deliver the needy when he crieth; the poor also, and him that hath no helper. And thus saith the high and lofty One, The heaven is my throne, and the earth is my footstool; but to this man will I look, that is poor and of a contrite heart, and that trembleth at my word." O, rely upon *that* Savior, and upon *these* promises, and the kingdom of God is yours in its present joys, and in its everlasting triumphs.

LECTURE III.

SECOND BEATITUDE.

"Blessed are they that mourn, for they shall be comforted." MATTHEW v, 4.

THIS is one of the most interesting of the beatitudes. It is a declaration full of tenderness and love, finding its way at once to the heart, and reviving hope where it had almost expired amid the glooms of despair. This is especially true when the soul is passing through the sorrows of penitence. Perhaps at no other time do doubts and fears weigh so heavily upon the heart. At no time is there such a depressing sense of helplessness. At no time is there such an anxious desire for relief; and, certainly, at no time are words of comfort so welcome to the bosom. Awakened to a sense of guilt, conscious of unpardoned sin and impending wrath, no wonder that alarm and terror overwhelms the soul. And when, too, at this period the light of the Spirit reveals the exceeding sinfulness of sin, the amazing goodness of God, and the extent and penalty of his law, no wonder if he should be driven to the very brink of despair. There was a time when he was easy and mirthful, but now a prisoner stretched upon the rack might pity him. The hand of God is on him, conviction like envenomed arrows pierces his heart; and a "wounded spirit who can bear?" How often have we heard such a one say, overborne with the burden of sin and the temptations of Satan, "Such a sinner as I am can not be pardoned; others may find comfort, but for me there is none. I have sinned so long and so greatly, my sins can never be blotted out; my guilt can never be washed away!"

Now, it is just at this point where the Savior meets us in his most gracious attitude. He had come from heaven upon an errand of encouragement, and with a heart full of compassion for the humble and the penitent. He knew the doubts and fears that beset the path of repentance, and like a merciful Savior as he is, sought to infuse strength, courage, and hope into the despairing sinner. How precious is his promise, how assuring are his words when he says, "Blessed are they that mourn, for they shall be comforted!" Whò would not wish to pass through the valley of mourning, with all its darkness and fear, to feel himself the inheritor of a promise so divine? Let us now,

I. Specify more particularly the characters to whom these words are applicable, "Blessed are they that mourn."

The Savior does not here intend all that mourn. Go out into the world, visit the abodes of men, every-where you find mourners; but, alas! not those whom he pronounces blessed. There are millions around us whose spirits are broken, and whose hearts bleed with sorrow. But theirs is the sorrow of the world, and to the world, as void of comfort as it is of God, they must turn for solace. Some are mourning from disappointed ambition; others from the stings of misfortune—the loss of property and the death of friends overwhelm them with sorrow. Others are detected in crime; their conduct is brought to light and exposed to the gaze of men, and they weep from fear of disgrace and ruin. All these pine in grief from mere worldly considerations. They have no proper views of sin; they do not feel themselves guilty, or look to God for pardon. Their sorrow arises from the world, and it terminates there. "It worketh death." Its present effects are gloom and distress; sometimes horrible despair. The spirit is wounded and the heart bleeds with grief, till finally the sufferer drops into the grave, or by self-destruction is hurried into the presence of a sin-avenging God. It is not to these the Savior speaks. They have no desire for the comfort he bestows. Could they call back their friends from the grave, or regain their reputation, or recall their wasted fortunes, it would be enough. They wish no higher comfort than the smiles of prosperity, and the applause of admiring friends. Alas! ye infatuated men, you will never know comfort. Your only doom is sorrow. Did you mourn for sin, your anguish would soon be turned to joy, and your bitter grief soon be followed by "the consolations of God."

These words are applicable to two classes of characters:

1. *The penitent sinner.*

He it is whom the Savior regards with the deepest compassion and love. "To *this* man will I look that is of a contrite heart, and that trembleth at my word." The true penitent mourns over sin—*his sin*—the fact, and the burden of which he has now a most painful consciousness. For years, perhaps, he was asleep in sin, *dead* in sin. He had no felt sense of his transgressions. Their guilt and enormity never excited his fears, or prompted a prayer for mercy. He still wandered from God, "walking according to the course of this world, fulfilling the desires of the flesh and of the mind, a child of wrath even as others." Privileges came and passed away, and left him still a sinner. Means and mercies plied him from week to week; but he abused them and grew harder. Thus he advanced in the way of sin. At length "he came to himself." The vail was torn from his heart. He was convinced of sin, and saw himself a guilty rebel in the sight of God. And now he begins to assume a character upon which heaven always looks with pity. He begins to mourn for sin. This discovery, however, is not the mere result of self-investigation; it is made by the Spirit of God. It is the effect of his light shining upon the soul, without which there is no true conviction for sin. And by conviction, I do not mean a bare knowledge of the fact that we have sinned; but such a knowledge as burdens and distresses the sinner. Such a conviction as the former may pass over the soul and scarcely ruffle its surface, while the latter will stir its very depths, and make it roll and dash like the ocean in a storm. For this end the Spirit was sent into the world; and when *he* reproves—when *he* flashes the light of truth upon the conscience, then, and only then does the sinner awake to the fact that he is a fallen spirit and in danger of hell.

Every thing in relation to himself now passes

through a great and rapid change. His own character—he had doted upon that, he had flattered himself upon the goodness of his heart, but he now sees the one sadly defective, and the other deceitful above all things, and desperately wicked. The number of his sins—the few admitted errors of his life now multiply to thousands, and in their sum are more than the hairs of his head. Their greatness—they have a greatness of guilt as well as of number, and while he contemplates them, they swell in dreadful enormity, and rise like mountains to the skies.

He now mourns over his sins as exposing him to hell. Alarm is an element of penitential sorrow. "The fear of the Lord is the beginning of wisdom;" the fear of his displeasure, "revealed from heaven against all unrighteousness and ungodliness of men." The Bible utters no truth more frequently or impressively, than the danger of sinners. It declares that they are "condemned already; that the wrath of God abideth on them; and that they shall be punished with an everlasting destruction." The fool and the hardened infidel mock at these declarations, and affect to despise them as childish fancies. Yet they themselves often shrink from the future with an instinctive dread "of judgment and fiery indignation." And well they may; for how dreadful is their doom, and how certainly will they perish, and "that without remedy!"

It is a sense of this danger that alarms the awakened sinner. He finds himself standing upon the very brink of woe. Justice rolls his thunders around his head, and threatens him with everlasting death. O, there is guilt upon his conscience, and he feels it as he would a crushing weight upon his body. O there is a deep and dreadful hell, and he fears its consuming fires! O, there is an insulted and displeased God, and he trembles lest he should cast him from his hand into the depths of endless perdition!

He mourns over his sins as committed against God. This is what St. Paul distinguishes as "godly sorrow, that worketh repentance unto salvation." This sorrow is exercised toward God in view of sin, and arises from a perception of the evil of sin as committed against a being of infinite goodness and purity. God is such a being. His goodness shines throughout the universe. From the firmament above, from all the valleys, and mountains, and groves of earth, voices speak and sing the goodness of the Lord. And in the wondrous plan of salvation, "he makes *all* his goodness to pass before us." His holiness is displayed in his word and law; in the nature of angels and the creation of man; in the sufferings of his Son, and in the office of the Holy Spirit. All these proclaim the infinite purity of God. Now, it is against this Being that sin is committed, and it is this that makes it so great an evil, and stamps the sinner with the most atrocious guilt. Such views of the Divine character result from the light and power of the Spirit; and when entertained, they touch the most secret springs of sensibility, and unlock the very *fountains* of feeling.

The source of grief at this particular stage of penitential experience, is not mainly that sin will lead to pain. that it will overwhelm the soul with everlasting ruin, but that it is committed against the Majesty of heaven, infinitely good, just, and holy. The penitent feels now that it was not only against law and authority that he raised his puny arm, but against goodness and mercy. It was *love* that he spurned; it was the tenderness of a *father* that he trampled upon. Such thoughts are like barbed arrows sticking fast, and as often as they return, wound the heart still deeper, and make it bleed afresh. Such were the feelings of David when he said, "Against thee only have I sinned and done this evil in thy sight." Enormous was the sin as committed against man, but all that enormity was lost in the greater guilt of being committed against infinite goodness and purity. This is the true light in which to view sin. As long as you regard it merely as an offense against man, your views will be imperfect, and it will seem but a trifling evil. But when, in the light of the Spirit, you see it an offense against God, then will it swell and blacken in all its malignity, and you will feel that "it is an evil and a bitter thing to sin against God."

This mourning derives much of its bitterness from the views which the penitent has of the sufferings of Christ. "They shall look upon me," says Christ by the prophet, "whom they have pierced, and they shall mourn for him as one mourneth for his only son, and shall be in bitterness for him, as one for his first-born." These allusions indicate the deepest sorrow. How inexpressible is the anguish of a man when he mourns for an only son, or is in bitterness for his first-born! Yet these are the terms employed by the Spirit to intimate something of that intense anguish which wrings the heart of a repentant sinner. But why such deepening sorrow? Ah! "he looks upon him whom he has pierced." He beholds the Savior upon the cross, bleeding and in agony What placed him there? My sins. Yes, these nailed him to the tree. My guilt sent the iron into his soul, and transfixed him to the cross. Hence springs the deepest sorrow of the mourning penitent. Looking thus on the Lord Jesus, they learn to feel and weep for sin, as they *alone* can who have looked upon him whom they have pierced. He who has not thus beheld that pierced and mangled form, who has no sense of the part he bore in that bloody tragedy, has no real grief for sin. A truly-broken heart he never felt. Do I now address such a one? O, how hard and cold is thy heart—hard as the rock, and cold as the ice of winter! And never will it break or melt till you look on the dying Jesus—never till you can say, He is bleeding for *me; I* pierced him; it is the burden of *my* sins that weighs down his fainting head.

His mourning is connected with confession for sin. Such grief is always ingenuous. He makes no attempt at concealment; he does not palliate or excuse himself; he frankly confesses and bewails his sins before God. This is always characteristic of the true penitent. Though ashamed and confounded at the number and greatness of his sins, he spreads them before the all-seeing eye of Jehovah. Before God and man he acknowledges his guilt. In private especially—the secluded grove, or silent chamber, he humbles himself before the Searcher of hearts, and fervently pleads for mercy. He has no reservations, but calmly unbosoms the painful conviction that he is utterly sinful in heart and life. He is not anxious to conceal the signs of distress. If his heart heaves with anguish, and his eyes overflow with tears, and his lips quiver with emotion, he does not assume an indifferent air; but, with sobs and tears, and often in a voice that all may hear, he confesses, with the prodigal, "Father, I have sinned against heaven, and in thy sight," or, with the publican, lifts the beseeching cry, "God be merciful to me a sinner."

True mourning for sin is fruitful. It leads to reformation; it is not mere regret, which, "like the morning cloud and early dew, passes away;" on the contrary, it produces visible and striking changes. A man who sees and mourns for sin as he ought will reform his life. He will cast from him, with loathing and disgust, even his best beloved sins; he will "break off his sins by righteousness, and his iniquities by turning to God." Such a man forsakes the company of the wicked, and the ways of evil men—he flies their approach as he would the plague or pestilence. Sin and sinful pleasures have lost their wonted charms and gorgeous robes, and now stand before him in their true character.

St. Paul traces these effects in the most graphic manner: "For behold this self-same thing, that ye sorrowed after a godly sort, what carefulness it wrought in you, yea, what clearing of yourselves, yea, what indignation, yea, what fear, yea, what vehement desire, yea, what zeal, yea, what revenge!" And these views harmonize with other parts of God's word. The abandonment of sin is universally and imperatively enjoined. "Cease to do evil, learn to do well; wash you, make you clean; put away the evil of your doings from before mine eyes;" "Let the wicked forsake his way, and the unrighteous man his thoughts;" "Now, saith the Lord, turn ye even unto me with all your heart, and with fasting, and with weeping, and with mourning; and rend your heart, and not your garments, and turn unto the Lord your God;" "Turn every man from his evil way, that I may repent me of the evil which I purpose to do unto them, because of the evil of their doings." Such is the language in which God urges upon men the abandonment of evil. And such a course invariably accompanies a genuine mourning for sin.

A most touching illustration of this character is given by St. Luke. The case was that of a woman—probably a woman of Capernaum or Nain. Her name is not given, but she was a repenting sinner, who, "when she knew that Jesus sat at meat in the Pharisee's house, brought an alabaster-box of ointment, and stood at his feet behind him weeping, and began to wash his feet with tears, and did wipe them with the hairs of her head, and kissed his feet, and anointed them with the ointment." Mark her position; overwhelmed with a sense of her unworthiness, she takes her station behind him, and at his feet. And what is her errand there? Perhaps to anoint his head, as the custom was, but diffidence restrains her. Her heart is melting under gracious influences; all she can do is to weep. Her tears flow like rain, so many and so fast, as to wash the Savior's feet. What a scene was this! Methinks an angel could not behold it without wishing to participate in its emotions. Weep, thou afflicted one, for thy sins thou *shouldst* weep; but thy tears shall yet be wiped away, and peace and joy shall balm thy wounded heart.

Some will, perhaps, say these were the tears of weakness and folly. Whence, then, the tears of the proud, imperious Manasseh—of the courageous and manly Peter? No; these are not the evidences of either weakness or folly, but of a humble and contrite heart. They are the outpourings of a heart mourning for sin, when it drinks the wormwood and gall of repentance. Thus must thou mourn for sin, or forever bear its guilt and punishment. Seest thou no cause for mourning? Look backward upon thy life—look forward to eternity. Look up to heaven, and down to hell. Seest thou yet no cause for mourning? Then think of the love of God and the compassions of Jesus. Go to Gethsemane, where he wept and prayed; go to Calvary, where he hung bleeding upon the cross. Think of his love and sorrow. Ah! think, till thy proud and stubborn heart shall break and bleed at the remembrance of sin.

2. *These words are also applicable to the Christian.*

They, too, mourn—not that religion is melancholy, or that it induces a sad and gloomy frame; no, it is peace and joy. Her ways are ways of pleasantness, and all who walk therein are happy. Yet there is a mourning eminently religious, and befitting Christian character—"as sorrowful, yet always rejoicing."

They often mourn under the adverse and afflictive

scenes of life. From the common lot of mortals religion gives no exemption. This world to the Christian is a stormy ocean, where tempests beat and billows roll. Disappointments, reverses, and trials, beset the toilsome way of life, and every fleeting day leaves behind a deeper conviction that man is born to trouble. The wants of poverty—personal affliction—bereavement of friends—the breaking up of the sweet and cherished endearments of conjugal and parental love; these sometimes roll over the heart like a wild deluge, sweeping away our dearest joys and brightest hopes. Like others, at such times the Christian mourns—with this difference, he is resigned and patient.

Besides the ordinary ills of life, there are those peculiar to the Christian. "Many are the afflictions of the righteous." "Through much tribulation he must enter the kingdom of heaven;" and he is sometimes "in heaviness through manifold temptations." Here he often mourns, for religion does not deaden the sensibilities or harden the heart. It rather gives a tender heart, perhaps that we may feel and weep, and seek that "better land" where all tears shall be wiped away.

They mourn in view of their imperfections and infirmities. He who sees none of these in himself, has the strongest evidence that he is alike ignorant of his own heart and of the operations of grace. No enlightened Christian, however holy he may be, can feel otherwise than that he is an unprofitable servant; and, conscious of unnumbered faults, he will often "write bitter things against himself." "When I reflect upon my sins," says the pious Baxter, "I find it much easier to believe that God will forgive me than I can forgive myself."

Renewing grace accomplishes much for the Christian. It delivers him from the guilt and dominion of sin. Under its almighty energies he becomes a "new creature;" "old things pass away and all things become new;" "he walks in newness of life," and advances toward perfection. Every power of the soul has felt the touches of transforming grace, and goes outward and upward to heaven and God. Thus a good work is begun; but there are many deficiencies; nor can he ever reflect upon them without mourning and humiliation. When he looks within, how much ingratitude does he see! What dullness and deadness! How little of love and zeal, of faith and power!

Follow the Christian to his place of retirement; see his tears, and mark the strugglings of his spirit. Hear his confessions: "O, my God, how oft have I wandered from thee—how many means have I neglected or misimproved—how many injuries have I done to others by my example and influence—how vain and worldly have I been—how prayerless and unwatchful! 'Pardon the iniquity of thy servant, and perfect that which concerneth me, O Lord.'" What Christian is not familiar with such scenes?

He mourns over the impenitence and wickedness of sinners. We can not even think of a Christian without thinking of one who is deeply affected with the guilt and woes of our fallen race. How unlike the Son of God would he be, who wept over the guilt and doom of Jerusalem! How unlike David, who said, "Rivers of water run down mine eyes, because they keep not thy law!"

Perhaps he is a minister; then he "goes forth weeping and sows in tears." How does he mourn over fruitless sermons and careless hearers! They seem to grow harder under his warnings, and blindly persist in sin. Such a minister was Paul: "I have told you often, and now tell you, even weeping, that they are the enemies of the cross of Christ." Such a minister was Jeremiah: "If ye will not hear," said he to the impenitent around him, "my soul shall weep in secret places for your pride; and mine eye shall weep sore, and run down with tears, because the Lord's flock is carried away captive."

Perhaps he is a relative. And can he "see the destruction of his kindred" without emotion? He is a father; around him rise his offspring. They are lovely and interesting, the objects of fond affection and unremitting toil; but they are fallen and sinful. They early show the tokens of depravity, the sad proofs of alienation from God. Unrenewed, they must perish. Can a pious father look upon them and not mourn—not ardently desire their salvation? No; they are the children of many prayers and tears; they are the objects of a solicitude that can never rest till they are brought within the fold of Christ. He is a husband, and mourns over the pride, vanity, and worldliness of a beloved wife. Or perhaps it is a pious wife, who mourns the impenitence of him on whose arm she leans. He to whom she looks for counsel and example, refuses to hear the word of life and turn from the ways of sin, and who, but for her prayers and tears, would long since have been "cut down as a cumberer of the ground."

But a Christian's sympathies reach beyond the circle of kindred and friends. A world is in ruins; millions are perishing around him; even while he surveys the appalling scene of a world lying in wickedness, thousands are hurried "from a life of sin to a state of punishment, and shriek to find themselves forever lost." As long as religion is love to God and man, a Christian must weep over such a world, where God is dishonored, the Savior despised, and immortal souls are lost. But this is a hallowed sorrow—it makes us like the Son of God, whose approbation and promise already encourage and cheer both the penitent and the believing heart. Let us now trace

II. THE APPLICATION OF THIS PROMISE TO THESE TWO CLASSES OF MOURNERS.

"Blessed are they, for they shall be comforted."

1. *Let us note its application to the case of the penitent sinner.*

In what sense are they blessed? Is not this a state of wretchedness, a condition of deep distress? Yes, they indeed drink the cup of wormwood, and the keen arrows of conviction transfix their hearts. Yet theirs is a gracious estate, and they are, therefore, blessed. It has been said, by some, "that the mourning of a penitent is but another form of rebellion, and springs from the enmity of the carnal mind." This doctrine is as false as it is pernicious, and dishonors the Savior as much as it discourages the penitent. Did he mourn because he was required to forsake his sins and "submit to God?"

because he was required to repent and believe in Christ? Then, indeed, would it be sinful. But he mourns because he has sinned, because he has insulted God and slighted the Savior; and it is right he should mourn, and repent in dust and ashes. And to encourage him therein the Savior regards him in pity, and assures him of approaching comfort. Penitential grief is an effect of grace, not of conflict with God; it is the result of divine illumination, and, if the heart yield to them, uniformly succeeds the visitations of the Spirit, when he "reproves of sin, of righteousness, and of judgment to come."

They shall be comforted.

God will graciously pardon the sins over which they now weep; "for he is nigh unto them that are of a broken heart, and saveth such as be of a contrite spirit." It is upon believing penitents that he looks with special regard. He will remove their burden, he will justify them through the blood of Christ, "blotting out their iniquities as a thick cloud from before him." Mark the assurances of his word: "Let the wicked forsake his way, and the unrighteous man his thoughts; and let him return unto the Lord, and he will have mercy upon him; and to our God, for he will abundantly pardon;" "I, even I, am he that blotteth out thy transgressions for mine own sake, and will not remember thy sins;" "Come," says Jesus, "unto me all ye that labor and are heavy laden, and I will give you rest." Such, O thou broken-hearted one, are the promises of thy God and Savior. Now, take an instance of their fulfillment: "I waited patiently for the Lord," says the royal penitent, "and he inclined unto me and heard my cry; he brought me up, also, out of a horrible pit, out of the miry clay, and set my feet upon a rock; and he hath put a new song in my mouth, even praises unto our God." Look up, then, in humble trust. Despair thou shouldst of thyself, but of infinite mercy never. Guilty and condemned thou art; but the tribunal of justice is changed into a throne of mercy. The Judge who sits there is the Savior of sinners, the very Savior who once hung bleeding upon the cross.

"Look up, thy broken heart prepare,
And God shall set the captive free."

They shall be comforted by the gift of the Holy Spirit. Of this he assures us in the language of promise: "He will give the Holy Spirit to them that ask him." And he is a comforter: this is both his name and office. His peculiar work is to dispel the clouds of unbelief—to apply the blood of atonement—to shed abroad the love of God in the heart, and witness to the fact and the extent of his work. As a Spirit of light he irradiates our darkness; as a Spirit of peace he calms the troubled bosom; and as a Spirit of adoption, with "sweet, persuasive voice,"

"He answers to the blood,
And tells me I am born of God."

Now the spirit of bondage vanishes, the crushing sense of guilt passes away, and the believing mourner, looking to heaven through his tears, says, with emotions no words can express, "O Lord, I will praise thee; for though thou wast angry with me, thine anger is turned away, and now thou comfortest me." And now, are any of you seeking this comfort—seeking it with a contrite heart? Then stretch forth the hand of faith and take it to your heart; it is rich and full, ay, more, it is free; it is offered, not because you are deserving of it, but for Christ's sake alone. Dost thou thus receive it? Then thy faith hath saved thee; go in peace.

2. *Equally applicable is this promise to mourning Christians.*

They, too, shall be comforted. Whatever may be the source of their grief or the weight of their affliction, the day of relief approaches, and its first beams already begin to kindle and glow amid the yielding darkness. Let us now make this a matter of personal interest.

Dost thou mourn under the adverse and afflictive scenes of life? And hast thou in faith and patience submitted thyself to the overruling providence of God? Then there is comfort for thee. The final result shall be far richer with joy, than the present is frought with sorrow. "All these things shall work together for good to them that love God." Thy reverses, thy poverty, thy bereavements shall eventuate well. A boundless, endless good shall evolve from seeming evil. Heavenly creations, bright with smiles, and glowing with immortal beauty, shall spring from the disorders of the present state. Then thou shalt bow and adore, or soar and sing, "Alleluia, for the Lord God omnipotent reigneth."

Art thou in heaviness through manifest trials and oppositions? Allow me simply to address you in the language of the Bible: "O thou afflicted, tossed with tempests and not comforted! behold, I will lay thy stones with fair colors, and lay thy foundations with sapphires. In righteousness shalt thou be established; thou shalt be far from oppression, for thou shalt not fear; and from terror, for it shall not come near thee." And mark the language of St. Paul: "The Lord shall deliver me from every evil work, and will preserve me unto his heavenly kingdom, to whom be glory forever and ever."

Dost thou mourn over thine imperfections and infirmities? So thou shouldst; so we are taught to pray and feel, before we commemorate the dying love of Christ. "We acknowledge and bewail our manifold sins and wickedness, which we have committed against thy divine Majesty." Though thou hast many imperfections both of heart and life, yet "cast not away thy confidence." "Hold that fast which thou hast;" comfort awaits thee. *Hope*, then, hope *largely*. Expect increasing measures of grace and spiritual power; for he who uttered these words upon the Mount of Blessing, intends to lead thee up to the highest elevations of Christian experience, where thou shalt rejoice in the full salvation of God. "Who hath despised the day of small things?" The spiritually proud and vainglorious may; but Jesus, blessings on his name! never will. "The bruised reed will he not break, and the smoking flax will he not quench." No, he will fan the feeble spark, and brace and strengthen the tender reed, till the one shall glow with living flame, and the other "flourish like a cedar in Lebanon." It is thus he will lead you on to perfection, if, while you mourn your remaining corruptions, you "lay aside every weight and the sin which doth so easily beset you." "For the Lord shall bruise Satan under your feet shortly. For this purpose was the Son of God manifested, that he might destroy the works of the devil. His name is Jesus; for he shall save his people from their sins." And now, in faith and hope, anticipate that period when thou shalt "walk in the comforts of the Holy Ghost," and the God of all comfort himself "shall fill and rule thy heart."

Or dost thou sigh and cry for the abominations of the land—for the sins of men, and for a perishing world? thou shalt be comforted. When, under discouragement and opposition, we prosecute an important enterprise, nothing tends more to strengthen and cheer the heart, than the assurance of final success. It relieves the present gloom and abates the force of present difficulties, to feel that whatever may happen we shall ultimately triumph over all opposition. Such is the position of the Christian. He weeps and labors, but his tears are preserved in the bottle of God, and his toils are written among the most precious records of heaven. All his mourning, all he has done and suffered in behalf of the Church and a sin-cursed world, shall ultimately be produced before assembled worlds, as the bright evidences of love to the Savior, and of his right to share the thrones and crowns of heaven. Thou weepest over the desolations of Zion! Look at the future. "Thine eyes shall see Jerusalem a quiet habitation, a tabernacle that shall not be taken down; not one of the stakes thereof shall ever be removed, neither shall any of the cords thereof be broken." Who, even while he bewails the sins of men, can read without a thrill of holy comfort the sublime strains of Isaiah: "Thy watchmen shall lift up the voice; with the voice together shall they sing: for they shall see eye to eye when the Lord shall bring again Zion. Break forth into joy, sing together, ye waste places of Jerusalem; for the Lord hath *comforted* his people, he hath redeemed Jerusalem. The Lord hath made bare his holy arm in the eyes of all nations; and all the ends of the earth shall see the salvation of our God." Weep thou mayest over the spreading sin and misery of the world, but not with a dark, distrustful heart. Look and wonder, and adore, as the bright scroll of prophecy unrolls before thine eyes; there I see "the forces of the Gentiles and the multitude of the isles converted to God;" I see "the house of the Lord established upon the tops of the mountains, and all nations flowing unto it." The desolations of the Church are rebuilt; "upon her walls is inscribed salvation, and upon her gates praise;" while from within a voice proclaims, "Thy sun shall no more go down; neither shall thy moon withdraw itself: for the Lord shall be thine everlasting light, and the days of thy mourning shall be ended."

"Come, ye disconsolate, where'er you languish;
Come, at the mercy-seat fervently kneel;
Here bring your wounded hearts, here tell your anguish;
Earth has no sorrow that heaven can not heal."

LECTURE IV.

THIRD BEATITUDE.

"Blessed are the meek, for they shall inherit the earth." MATTHEW v, 5.

In two things especially Christianity exhibits its superior excellence—the sublimity of its doctrines, and the purity of its precepts; and had it no other marks of a heavenly origin, these would be sufficient to authenticate its claims and establish its truth as a revelation from God. In regard to its precepts, their purity is abundantly manifest from what they require of man. They have, first, a general character; they spread over the whole field of human duty, and lay their commanding force upon the entire life and deportment of man. They are, also, particular and special; they are adapted to every circumstance and department in human life; and are especially directed to the tempers and dispositions of the heart. The design is apparent; it was to form a character, at once so new and lovely, as to impress and convince every succeeding age of the truth and divinity of the Christian religion.

In this character the mild and retiring virtues chiefly prevail. The sterner virtues are indeed present; but among those that shine with a holier luster we may see gentleness, patience, and meekness. It is upon these religion sets the highest value, enjoins by the most commanding authority, and encourages by the most delightful promises. Such views, however, are very different from those entertained by the world. Meekness, for example, has no place in its code of honor or its list of virtues. It is usually regarded as a proof of weakness, and the sure indication of a little mind; while the spirit that can revenge an insult and crush an enemy, is the subject of applause, and gives its possessor the character of a hero; and yet, whatever may be the judgment of the world, the meek have the especial regards of the Savior. The manner in which he brings this character before us in the text, is ample proof of this: "*Blessed* are the meek, for they shall inherit the earth."

But what is meekness? In ordinary language, it signifies softness of temper; forbearance under injuries and provocations. In an evangelical sense, it signifies humility, resignation, submission to the Divine will, without murmuring or peevishness, and stands opposed to pride, arrogance, and sullen obstinacy; as such, it is purely the result of regenerating grace. It is not to be confounded with constitutional gentleness and equanimity; this may exist where the power of renewing grace is unknown. The natural tempers of men vary much; some are calm and quiet, others fiery and passionate; some sit unmoved amid circumstances that enrage others beyond control; some are tender and forgiving, and others harsh and revengeful. As in the one case there can be no claim to Christian meekness, it may be equally so in the other. Each may exhibit only the natural temper and inclination of the heart.

The meekness of which the Savior speaks, is

founded in poverty of spirit; it is eminently a fruit of the Spirit—the offspring of pure religion; it is a distinguishing trait of the true Christian, who, having "put off the old man, has put on the new man, which is renewed after the image of God." And now, from that heart, where pride once reigned and passion poured its fiery torrents, the pure and gentle stream of meekness flows, spreading cheerfulness and verdure wherever it comes. Abiding as a principle in the renewed heart, its precious fruits are displayed in all the circumstances, relations, duties, and pursuits of life. We shall now,

I. In the first place, delineate the character of the meek.

And may He who was himself the great pattern of meekness, divinely aid us in our attempt!

1. *The readiness and docility with which they receive the doctrines of the Gospel, form a leading characteristic of the meek.*

They do not read or hear the word of God in the spirit of criticism or censoriousness, but in the spirit of candor, and with a sincere desire to know his will. The proud and conceited approach the divine word with very different feelings, inflated with the idea of their own superior wisdom, and charmed with the lights of science, falsely so called; they ridicule the doctrines of the Gospel, and pronounce, with the confidence of unerring wisdom, upon the sublime mysteries and precepts of religion. Such vanity renders them unfit to investigate its claims or appreciate its worth. To do either, they must descend from the giddy hights of self-conceit; they must cast away the pride of reason, and bow down before the majesty of truth; then shall they realize that God "will guide the meek in judgment, and the meek will he teach his way."

There are those, too, who, from passion mixed with pride, lift a bold and stubborn front of opposition to the teachings of Christ. To be called a sinner—a child of wrath—an heir of hell, wounds their feelings; it is a gross insult, and sets the soul in a blaze of passion. Truth can never enter such a heart as this. Passion has barred the entrance, and stands defiant upon the threshold. If the Gospel ever enter there it must be received with meekness. "Wherefore," says an inspired apostle, "lay apart all filthiness and superfluity of naughtiness." These comprehend that "wrath of man," to which he had just alluded, "which worketh not the righteousness of God." Such a state of mind is unfavorable to the reception of truth. "And receive with meekness the ingrafted word, which is able to save your souls." A subdued and tranquil spirit, open to instruction, and wishing for light, is alone fitted to see the beauty of religion, to appreciate its value and understand its instructions.

"Meekness," says Matthew Henry, "breaks up the fallow ground, and makes it fit to receive the seed. It captivates the high thoughts, and lays the soul like white paper under God's pen. Meekness softens the wax, that it may receive the impression of the seal, whether it be for doctrine or reproof, for correction or instruction in righteousness. It opens the ear to discipline, it silences objections, and quells the risings of the carnal mind against the word of God."

It is in the manner thus indicated the meek receive the announcements of infinite wisdom. Deeply penetrated with a sense of their own ignorance and sin, they are *willing* to be taught. They listen to the voice of God, and yield themselves to the guidance of his Spirit. They believe its statements, and welcome to their bosoms its bright and searching beams. That system of heavenly truth which enlightens the understanding, sanctifies the heart, and consoles the spirit, they now embrace with exceeding joy. Such a man goes to the Bible, not for advice but law. He is willing to abide the verdict of God. He does not dictate, he does not prescribe, but he says, "I will hear what God the Lord will speak." And he kneels and prays, "Lord, I believe, help thou mine unbelief."

2. *The meek are resigned and submissive under the dispensations of divine Providence.*

St. Paul is a fine example. "I have learned," says he, "in whatsoever state I am, therewith to be content." We see it beautifully exemplified in the conduct of David. A dark providence had overwhelmed him with affliction; he fled before Absalom, his rebel son, who had conspired against his kingdom and sought his life. A few chosen men, with the priests and Levites bearing the holy ark, followed him in his exile. Having passed the brook, he turned to the priest, and with meek resignation said, "Carry back the ark; if I find favor in the eyes of the Lord, he will show me both it and his habitation; but if he say I have no delight in thee, behold here am I, let him do to me as seemeth good unto him."

The dispensations of divine Providence are often mysterious and trying. "His way is in the sea and his path in the great waters;" "Clouds and darkness are round about him," and no human sagacity can comprehend his ways or penetrate his "bright designs." How often, under such circumstances, do men arraign the wisdom of God, and charge him with ignorance and cruelty; or, if not sufficiently bold for such daring impiety as this, they fret under the corrections of his hand, and murmur at those events which seem to thwart their purposes and plans! From one he takes away property, from another health, from a third family or friends. He deranges our plans, hedges up our way, and throws dark shadows upon our course; and, as far as we can see, without reason or necessity. This is the precise point where

"Blind unbelief is sure to err."

The soul starts up in rebellion, and, if it does not blaspheme, utters the language of complaint: "All these things are against me." The small voice that speaks, "Be still, and know that *I* am God," is unheard or unheeded amid the tumult of excited feeling, or the strugglings of unhumbled pride.

The distinction is wide and deep between such a rebel spirit and the calm submission of the meek. Acknowledging the supremacy of God and his right to rule the universe, they bow to his authority, and resign themselves to his all-wise disposal. They are not indifferent to reverses or insensible to suffering. They feel, perhaps, more keenly than others, the trials and sorrows of life, but they neither murmur nor repine. Their spirit and temper is beautifully exemplified in the conduct of Job, who, when bereft of his children, and stripped of every earthly possession, fell upon the ground and worshiped, saying, "The Lord gave, and the Lord hath taken away: *blessed* be the name of the Lord!"

A touching incident, and beautifully illustrative of Christian meekness, is related by Capt. Carlton in his memoirs. It occurred at the siege of Barcelona, in 1705. "An old and pious officer, having his only son, a most promising boy, with him, sat down in the tent to dine. While thus engaged, a shot from one of the bastions took off the head of his son. The father immediately rose up, first looking down upon his headless and bleeding child, and then lifting his eyes to heaven, while the tears ran in streams down his cheeks, only said, *Father, thy will be done!*"

Such is true Christian meekness. It never doubts the wisdom of Providence, or foolishly charges his administration. Whatever storms may disturb the elements—whatever calamities may lower or burst upon it, meekness calmly and sweetly sinks into the will of God, and rests in security beneath the shadow of his wings.

3. *The meek are calm and patient under offenses and provocations.*

Perhaps no where does divine grace display itself with more beauty and power than in this amiable temper. It properly denotes that state of mind which can *bear long* when provoked and calumniated. It, therefore, stands in direct opposition to irritability; to a hot and hasty spirit, venting itself in angry thoughts and words. It is one of the gentle offsprings of charity, a heaven-born principle, and, like its celestial parent, is always benignant. "It beareth all things, endureth all things, is not easily provoked," but keeps the spirit calm and unruffled amid persecution and ill-usage. "The effect of religion," says one, "is no where more striking and apparent than in changing a temper, naturally quick and excitable, to one that is calm, and gentle, and subdued." If any thing *can* indicate the presence and power of the Holy Spirit *this* does; and both the presence and the power of that divine agent are necessary in the formation of this temper. A man is not meek simply because he endures—his endurance may arise from other causes. With some it may be indolence, with others insensibility, and with a third class constitutional fortitude. Christian meekness is ever a "fruit of the Spirit," and is exercised under insult and injury, in obedience to God, and for the honor of his holy name.

Many persons are petulant and irritable; every spark inflames them; they can bear nothing; hardly a day passes in which some occurrence does not wound their pride and insult their dignity; they fancy that every man's hand is against them; and yet the whole secret of their troubles lies in the fact that they are "easily provoked." "It must needs be that offenses come." So various are the characters and tempers of men, so conflicting often their interests and pursuits, that they will inevitably arise. How supremely miserable must they be who are thus passionate! There is no more certain way to imbitter life and poison every stream of happiness, than to indulge an unkind and sour temper. Nothing contributes so much to alienate the affections of a husband, a wife, a friend; and nothing will sooner banish smiles and contentment from the family circle or break it up in fragments.

On the contrary, how delightful is the influence of the quiet virtues of patience and forbearance! They are refreshing as the dews of heaven; they gladden and cheer the circle of their influence like the gentle rivulet that flows on day and night, clothing its banks with verdure and flowers. What an adorning is the meek and quiet spirit to the husband, the wife, the brother, the sister, the friend, the neighbor! Such a one "is no brawler, but gentle, showing all meekness to all men;" "he is slow to wrath, knowing that the wrath of man worketh not the righteousness of God." The salutary effects of this spirit are seen especially in its power over the harsh and oppressive. It subdues the passionate and calms the stormy spirit, sometimes even melting it into contrition and tears. "A soft answer turneth away wrath." The history of the meek furnishes many beautiful illustrations of this. "A husband, in a moment of passion, said to her whom, but a few months before, he had promised to love and honor, 'If you are not satisfied with my conduct, go, return to your friends and your happiness!' 'And will you give me back that which I brought to you?' asked the weeping wife. 'Yes,' he replied, 'all your wealth shall go with you, I covet it not.' 'Alas!' she answered, 'I thought not of wealth; I spoke of my maiden affections—of my buoyant hope—of my devoted love; can you give these back to me? 'No,' said the subdued husband, now throwing himself at her feet, 'no, I can not restore these; but I will do more—I will keep them unsullied and unstained; I will cherish them through life!'"

Such, under insult and reproach, is the spirit of meekness. He who by grace possesses it, esteems it the glory of a man to pass by a transgression; he is gentle and patient; "he is not overcome of evil, but overcomes evil with good;" he has learned the art of self-government, he can command himself. Such a man is a victor and a hero, "above all Greek, all Roman fame;" "for he that is slow to anger is better than the mighty, and he that ruleth his spirit than he that taketh a city."

4. *Their readiness to forgive injuries as well as to bear them patiently, is another characteristic of the meek.*

On this subject the maxims of the world and the precepts of the Gospel are in direct variance. The language of a distinguished philosopher fitly expresses the views of men in every age: "It is good to avenge ourselves upon our enemies; for it is but just to return the same measure that we have received." How different is the lesson which the meek Son of God taught his disciples! On one occasion Peter approached him with this question, "Lord, how often shall my brother offend against me and I forgive him? till seven times? Jesus replied, I say not unto thee, till seven times, but till seventy times seven." This precept is peculiar to the religion of Christ; it is not found in Pagan philosophy or in any other system of morals. The prominence given it by our Savior is remarkable. Every harsh and unforgiving temper—every thing like a feeling of resentment, however popular in the world, is forbidden, as inconsistent with the spirit of his religion. His coming into the world was the result of infinite love, and his own example in the exercise of pardon must be followed by his disciples, or he will disown them before his Father and the holy angels. Let us ponder for a moment the nature and bearings of this sublime precept. 1. It does not mean that we are to be insensible to injuries. Religion is designed to control and regulate, not to annihilate the constitutional principles of our being. 2. It does not mean that we are to approve the conduct of the injurious; for if it be wrong, we neither can nor ought to approve it. 3. It does not mean that we are to regard them with complacency; for if their characters are bad, this would be wrong; and if our hearts are right, it is impossible. It means, 1. That under no circumstances are we to harbor malice against them. 2. We are to be ready to do them good, to extend to them acts of kindness as we have opportunity. 3. We are to stand ready to declare our forgiveness when they ask us. 4. We are thereafter to treat them with affectionate kindness, as if they had not offended us. Thus God acts toward us. "Forbearing one another, and forgiving one another," says the apostle, "if any man have a quarrel against any: even as Christ forgave you, so also do ye." "The force of this motive," says the pious Bishop Wilson, "it is impossible fully to appreciate. Our faults are without number, our guilt inexcusable, our misery helpless; and yet Christ forgave us; and at what a price!—his incarnation, his sacrifice, his blood, his bitter death upon the cross." This godlike disposition does not flow from meanness or cowardice, nor does it consist in a surrender of our rights; but it is the opposite of sudden anger—of malice—of long-harbored vengeance. Christ insisted on his rights, when he said, "If I have done evil, bear witness of the evil, but if well, why smitest thou me?" Paul asserted his right when he said, "They have beaten us openly uncondemned, being Romans, and have cast us into prison; and now do they thrust us out privily? nay, verily; but let them come themselves and fetch us out." And yet Christ was *the model* of meekness. With the highest degree of truth he could say, I am meek and lowly. So of Paul; yet they were not passionate; they did not harbor malice; they were not unforgiving; they did not press their rights through thick and thin, and trample down the rights of others to secure their own. Readiness to forgive injuries, then, must ever be regarded as characteristic of the meek. They cherish no hate and indulge no feelings of resentment; they are mild and gentle; conscious of their own unnumbered offenses, they are ever ready to forgive the offenses of others.

"How beautifully falls
From human lips that blessed word, *forgive!*"

Its exercise is true magnanimity, and more than any thing beside ennobles and adorns the character of man.

5. *The meek are also distinguished by the affectionate kindness with which they treat an erring brother.*

"Brethren," says an apostle, "if a man be overtaken in a fault, ye which are spiritual restore such a one in the spirit of meekness." And, again, we read, "In meekness instructing those that oppose themselves; if God peradventure will give them repentance to the acknowledging of the truth." This trait was exemplified in the conduct of St. Paul, in the most lovely manner. Instead of a harsh and commanding air, he says to the Thessalonians, "We were gentle among you, even as a nurse cherisheth her children." How tender is the solicitude which a mother feels for the infant reposing upon her bosom! The instruction she imparts, the reproof and correction she administers are all prompted by ardent and glowing love. So Paul felt, and in this spirit he sought to win men to Christ. But the most lovely and striking illustration ever given to the world was in the conduct of our blessed Savior; it was characteristic of all he said and did in behalf of erring men. True, he spoke with authority; he pronounced the most awful threatenings; but they were the utterances of mercy, and came from a heart overflowing with love. To instruct and restore the wandering sinner is the godlike work of Christians. We are workers together with him; we are to work like him; and as gentleness and love marked his conduct toward even the worst of men, we are to be governed by the same principles in our efforts to do good. Affectionate kindness will melt and win when nothing else can. Hearts as hard as iron have been fused under the persuasions of Christian love, while the yielding conscience has been changed to adamant by an overbearing, imperious manner. Christian meekness is always kind and serene; it selects a proper time and place; it reproves with authority and truthfulness, but with all long-suffering, showing all meekness to all men. It is not rude but gentle; it subdues by tenderness, and compels by the resistless eloquence of love. Its words fitly spoken, "are like apples of gold in baskets* of silver." They enter the heart "like goads, and are as nails fastened by the Master of assemblies."

Such, then, are some of the more obvious traits of the meek; and how amiable and lovely is this character! "They are followers of God;" "They have the mind which was in Christ." Angels glowing in the beauty of holiness, and shining in the splendor of heaven, do not more resemble the Son of God than they. Do you admire this character? then imitate it. The world may admire the brave and fearless disputant, the brawling polemic, but "the wrath of man worketh not the righteousness of God." Be it yours and mine, my brethren, to cultivate "that meek and quiet spirit, which in the sight of God is of great price." This will crown us with the favor of God, and constitute us fellow-heirs with the meek in the wealth of a present and imperishable estate. "Blessed are the meek, *for they shall inherit the earth.*"

II. LET US NOW INVESTIGATE THE NATURE OF THIS PROMISE.

Some expositors have applied it exclusively to the present world; others to the future and heavenly inheritance. Its application, however, should embrace both the one and the other. This is certainly

* The learned say the original allows this rendering, and it is preferable to the common version.

more in harmony with the general sense of the Bible. The encouragements of piety are indeed chiefly the hope of spiritual blessings, yet they are sometimes temporal also; for "godliness hath the promise of the life that now is, as well as that which is to come." The words are perhaps a quotation from the thirty-seventh Psalm, and the connection there indicates that its application to temporal, as well as spiritual good, was the design of the inspired penman.

The phrase, "inherit the earth," relates not so much to the largeness and wealth of their possessions, as to the enjoyment of what Providence has given them. It means to *enjoy* rather than to possess. This is the essential idea. Do vast estates produce corresponding happiness? When men inherit largely do they enjoy in the same proportion? Never. The rule is the reverse of this; enjoyment is the exception. Few, however, believe this till they have wasted life in experiments; yet all experience, as well as the words of Christ, unite in declaring that "a man's life consisteth not in the abundance of the things which he possesseth." No. Many a man without a fixed abode or certain daily bread, enjoys more than he who rolls in all the plenty of wealth. He alone really inherits the earth who enjoys it; and that enjoyment, singular as it may seem, depends upon conditions which the mere possession can never supply. This inheritance, then, may exist amid poverty, and be a richer portion than vast domains or coffers filled with gold. This promise, then, secures,

1. *Temporal advantages.*

In regard to the present life, they have an interest

in the benevolent provisions of Providence. "The wise of the world," in the language of Mr. Wesley, "had warned them that if they did not resent affronts, if they would tamely suffer abuse, they could expect no peace, no quiet possession, no enjoyment of any thing. Most true, if there were no God in the world, or if he did not concern himself in the affairs of men; but when God ariseth to judgment, and to help all the meek of the earth, how doth he laugh all this heathen wisdom to scorn, and turn the fierceness of man to his praise! He takes a peculiar care to provide them with all things needful for life and godliness; he secures to them the provisions he has made, despite the force, fraud, or malice of men; and what he secures he gives them richly to enjoy. It is sweet to them; they are contented—pleased with what they have. So that while their heart and their joy is in heaven, they may be truly said to inherit the earth."

We may derive an illustration of this promise from a descriptive phrase of St. Paul, applied to himself and others: "As having nothing and yet possessing all things." This is peculiarly applicable to the meek. In the knowledge of the Redeemer and the friendship of God he possesses all things. This comprehends all; he can want no more; this satisfies the soul, and renders it supremely happy; "for if God spared not his own Son, but delivered him up for us all, how shall he not with him also freely give us all things?" That portion of all things which a wise and beneficent Father sees necessary, is freely bestowed. He has such an interest in them as to enjoy them; and he can say, as his eye sweeps over the spreading glories of creation, "*My Father* made them all." They are his, in that he can contemplate them, and see in them the brilliant proofs of a Father's infinite wisdom and goodness. As he looks upon the hills and vales of earth, its placid lakes and flowing streams, its fruitful farms and enchanting landscapes, he feels a pleasure unknown to their proud and haughty owner. He claims them as a child and heir of God—a claim of higher value than title deeds convey.

They who can realize an interest in the wealth of Him who made and owns the universe, can never be called poor; "all things are theirs." And in their humble abodes, and with their scanty fare, they have an enjoyment of the earth unknown in the palaces and at the tables of the rich. The wicked may flourish in the earth; they may inherit large estates; they may measure their domains by leagues, and count their treasures by millions; but all their possessions are by sufferance; they are tenants at will, and liable any moment to ejectment. "I have seen," says the Psalmist, "the wicked in great power, and spreading himself like a green bay-tree. Yet he passed away, and, lo, he was not; yea, I sought him, but he could not be found." "For evildoers shall be cut off; but those that wait upon the Lord, they shall inherit the earth." The meek possess by inheritance; they are the legatees of heaven; all their blessings are the gift of a father's love. As the children of God, no reverses can deprive them of their enjoyments; they are held by a tenure which no fraud can violate, no vicissitudes impair.

Furthermore, this promise secures exemption from

many of the disquietudes of life. One of the most prolific sources of trouble to men are their own restless and unsanctified tempers. Pride, impatience, and a hasty spirit, are enough to imbitter life aside from other causes. They are like a thorn in the flesh, or like burning coals in the bosom. He who possesses them can never be at rest; he is tormented with a thousand vexations, that exist only in his own imagination. The pleasures of others render him unhappy, even as the pleasant light of heaven frets and pains the eye inflamed and sensitive by disease. The meek escape these ever-recurring disquietudes. His gentleness prevents instead of causes occasions of pain. Kindness disarms his enemies, and binds his friends with a purer and stronger attachment. His sweetness of temper neutralizes the acid and gall with which he daily comes in contact, and covers him as with a shield against the darts of malice and the stings of slander. If he has erred, he meekly confesses it; if he has suffered an injury, meekness leads him to receive an acknowledgment and forgive the offender. In this manner he passes through the world; the gales of passion that agitate the multitude are unfelt by him; the disappointments and rebuffs that sting the petulant to madness harm him not.

> "He bears himself
> So gently, that the lily on its stalk
> Bends not so easily its dewy head."

Such a temper relieves life of half its burdens. Like the healing wood of Moses, it sweetens the waters of bitterness, and turns them to sources of refreshment along the weary deserts of life.

In fine, when troubles arise, the meek are not affected by them as others. I have seen the mighty oak riven and prostrated by the tempest, while the pliant reed, meekly bending to the blast, received no injury. And thus have I seen the proud and haughty overwhelmed by sorrow—crushed and broken down by earthly calamity; while the meek, submissive Christian, borne up amid his trials, has lived to smile and flourish when the storm had passed away. The vicissitudes of life, whether for good or evil, he receives as from the hand of God. To his will he cheerfully resigns himself. His way he commits to the Lord, trusting also in him, assured that his righteousness shall be brought forth as the light, and his judgment as the noonday. He rejoices in present safety. Troubles may arise, but he stands on a rock, "joyful in tribulation; knowing that tribulation worketh patience, and patience experience, and experience hope." Like the great Luther, he can sit and sing amid the storm, "*God* is our refuge and strength, a very present help in trouble. Therefore will not we fear, though the earth be removed, and though the mountains be carried into the midst of the sea; though the waters thereof roar and be troubled; though the mountains shake with the swelling thereof."

2. *This promise looks beyond the present state, and secures an everlasting inheritance.*

It was probably taken from that made to the Israelites. The promise was that they and their posterity should inherit the land of Canaan. In the glowing language of the East, it was described as "a land of corn and wine, as flowing with milk and honey, and as the glory of all lands." This land was an eminent and beautiful type of the heavenly Canaan, the "land which is afar off, where the king shall be seen in his beauty," when the weary pilgrimage of life is over. "To the meek, therefore," says Mr. Watson, "the inheritance of heaven is here promised, and none but the meek shall inherit it; for without this most essential branch of holiness no man shall see the Lord."

Beyond Jordan lies the rich inheritance—a pleasant and a goodly land, where "the inhabitants never say they are sick, and where the weary are at rest." All evil is far away, and all that is good is there. No change comes there, no sickness, no death, no grief, no wasting remorse, no bitter memory, no secret sting. No trumpet of war resounds through its groves, no enemy lurks in the shelter of its palmy trees, no scorching wind from the desert withers its immortal flowers. Of this bright world the meek are heirs; they have become such by grace; but they are now in their minority, under many restraints, and subject to a course of discipline, the reasons of which are not always apparent. They must bear the cross, exercise self-denial, and sometimes endure chastisement; but they are advancing to maturity, and the period of investiture is at hand. How imposing the final scene, when the meek shall be exalted and crowned! "Before the Son of Man shall be gathered all nations, and he shall say to them upon his right hand, Come ye blessed of my Father, inherit the kingdom prepared for you from the foundation of the world." They approach; the gates unfold, and they enter. Heaven glows with a brighter radiance and rings with sweeter songs; for the ransomed of the Lord have gained their inheritance—"an inheritance, incorruptible, undefiled, and that fadeth not away."

CONCLUSION.

I can not close these observations, without submitting a few directions in reference to the cultivation of Christian meekness.

First of all, begin right. As meekness is pre-eminently a fruit of the Spirit, it can only exist in a regenerate heart. Begin, then, by seeking the renewing grace of God. Not till you are a new creature in Christ Jesus may you hope to possess this heavenly temper. The bramble does not bear grapes, nor the thistle figs, nor does an evil and unholy heart bring forth the fruit of meekness. Seek, then, "the washing of regeneration and the renewing of the Holy Ghost, which" alone can purify the heart and fill it with divine affections. Pray, ever pray, "Create in me a clean heart, O God, and renew a right spirit within me."

Guard your tempers; these, like roots of bitterness, will spring up and trouble you. Moving as you do amid scenes of conflict and provocation, the least you can do is to watch. Be sober, be vigilant; guard against the outbreaks of passion. You carry within you materials, which the sparks of strife may kindle into consuming fires. "Keep thy heart with all diligence, for out of it are the issues of life." Shut every gate, bar every door, and close every avenue through which passion has been wont to enter. As you regard your peace, as you dread satanic malice, set a sleepless watch over your heart.

Aspire to imitate the example of the Son of God. All others have their spots and blemishes, but his example is perfection itself. In his meekness, resignation, and forgiving love, he is the exact model of what we should become. "Learn of me," is his beautiful command, "for I am meek and lowly." Learn as the scholar from his copy; *imitate* him. This, Christian, is your high calling, your elevated privilege. Pause not till the meekness and gentleness of Christ pervades your heart, and invests your character as with a robe and a diadem of glory.

To all this add prayer; ask of God this divine adorning; seek the presence and power of restraining grace. "When you are angry," says one, "answer not till you have prayed, 'Forgive us our trespasses as we forgive them that trespass against us.'" The exercise of devotion will check resentment, hush the storm of passion, and diffuse through the soul the serenity of heaven itself. May you cultivate this spirit; and may you realize, now and through all your future being, the blessedness of its attainment!

LECTURE V.

FOURTH BEATITUDE.

"Blessed are they which do hunger and thirst after righteousness: for they shall be filled." MATTHEW v, 6.

THERE is much in the sinful heart to hinder the beginning and the progress of religion. It is ruled by the spirit of darkness; it is full of enmity to God—an enmity that never yields without a struggle, and can only be slain by the power of divine grace. Particular evils offer resistance; among the more prominent we may observe pride, impenitence, and passion. These, from their very nature, must ever oppose the entrance of light and life into the soul. Pride will not acknowledge its wants, impenitence will not bewail its sins, nor passion submit itself to God. While these enemies stand upon the threshold of the heart, religion will not, *can not* enter. Pride must sit down in the dust; impenitence must weep and mourn, for sin and passion must sink in meekness at the feet of Christ. Then, and only then, is the way open for the sublime work of religion.

To effect this was one design of the Savior in the preceding beatitudes. "Blessed," says he, "are the poor in spirit; blessed are they that mourn; blessed are the meek." These several states of mind are in the highest degree favorable to the progress and perfection of religion. Beginning in the dust with utter emptiness and poverty, he gradually advances and ascends till every obstruction is removed, and religion reigns and triumphs upon the throne of the heart.

This beatitude is eminently encouraging. It was evidently not intended to apply to any one blessing, or any particular stage of Christian experience, but to each and all without distinction. It would certainly be an error to limit its application in the least, when every sincere seeker of the kingdom of God so much needs its encouraging assurance. Every seeker of religion, every penitent imploring pardon, every believer desiring a growth in grace, and panting for the full salvation of God, has a right to claim it as his own. Is he in earnest? Does he hunger and thirst? If so, then he is welcome to the fullness, and is entitled to claim all that it means, both for the present and the future world. "Blessed," then, "are they which do hunger and thirst," not after earthly good, but "after righteousness: for they shall be filled." God himself shall supply their need, and satisfy their desires with the fullness of redeeming grace. Let us now consider,

I. The nature of that righteousness of which our Savior speaks.

Few words in the Bible are more various in their import than the word righteousness; its meaning, however, may be readily ascertained by keeping in view its connections and applications. It is sometimes applied to God, and then signifies not only his justice, but the absolute and essential holiness of his nature. Sometimes it is applied to the blessed Redeemer in his personal and mediatorial character, and then, again, we read of "the righteousness of the law," which consists in uniform obedience to its precepts as a perfect rule of life. In the text it has a very different application. Mr. Watson, in his note upon this passage, says, "Righteousness is to be taken in the sense of holiness, which consists in the entire renewal of the soul after the image of God." And Dr. Clarke says, that the word is to be taken "for all the blessings of the new covenant—all the graces of the Messiah's kingdom—a full restoration to the image of God." Righteousness, then, properly signifies *inward religion*—the whole of that divine work in the soul which prepares it for a habitation of God through the Spirit, and for the future and final abodes of the glorified in heaven. As an object of desire and pursuit it comprehends,

1. *Pardon, or the forgiveness of our actual transgressions.*

This is the righteousness of faith, and becomes ours not by any transfer of the righteousness of Christ to us—for moral character can not be transferred—nor by its being infused into us, but by the pardon of our sins through faith in Jesus Christ. Thus was Abraham, the father of the faithful, constituted righteous. He believed God, and it was counted to him for righteousness. "To him," says St. Paul, "that worketh not, but believeth on him that justifieth the ungodly, his faith is counted for righteousness; even as David describeth the blessedness of the man unto whom God imputeth righteousness without works, saying, Blessed are they whose iniquities are forgiven, and whose sins are covered; blessed is the man to whom the Lord will not impute sin." The deduction which the apostle makes from this fine argument fixes the sense of the entire connection: "Therefore, being justified by faith, we have peace with God through our Lord Jesus Christ." The pardon of sin, righteousness without works, and justification by faith, imply the same thing—the forgiveness of our sins. Our guilt is now canceled, our iniquities are carried away into a land of forgetfulness, and we are henceforth treated as the friends of God.

Now, to each and all of you is this righteousness offered. God commands and invites you to seek it; and he offers to bestow it upon you all if you will cast yourselves upon the merits of his Son, and "believing with a heart unto righteousness." The world does not present an object of desire worthy of comparison with this. To you, a fallen man, a ruined sinner, and even now condemned to death, can there be any thing of equal importance? How you may escape the coming wrath, how your sins may be blotted out, how you may find mercy with God, are questions of vast and everlasting concern—questions that should awake infinite desires, and call forth all your powers in pursuit.

2. *It comprehends personal regeneration.*

By this I do not mean mere reformation of life—the abandonment of overt wickedness. Men may do this; they may go further—they may adopt such principles and pursue such a line of conduct as shall win the applause of all that know them, and yet remain under the full sway of that carnal mind which is enmity to God. Outward reformation is not enough; you must go beyond this if you would be righteous before God. The ancient Pharisees assumed even a profession of religion; they were exact in all outward forms; they prayed long and often; they paid tithes of all; and yet said the Savior to his disciples, "Except your righteousness exceed the righteousness of the scribes and Pharisees, ye shall in no case enter into the kingdom of heaven." And so, we may assume the badge of Christian discipleship, and go far in the externals of religion, and yet remain in the gall of bitterness and in the bonds of iniquity.

By regeneration I mean the production of spiritual life in him who was dead in trespasses and sins. In the language of Mr. Watson, "It is that mighty change in man, wrought by the Holy Spirit, by which the dominion which sin has over him in his natural state, and which he deplores and struggles against in his penitent state, is broken and abolished, so that, with full choice and the energy of right affections, he serves God freely, and runs in the way of his commandments." These views fully harmonize with the word of God. "You hath he quickened," says St. Paul, "who were dead in trespasses and sins;" "If any man be in Christ he is a new creature; old things have passed away; behold, all things are become new;" "Whosoever," says St. John, "is born of God doth not commit sin; for his seed remaineth in him, and he can not sin, because he is born of God." This change, then, is no superficial thing; it is no partial or temporary interruption in the character and tendencies of the moral feelings; but a change of heart so thorough as to be fitly represented by a new birth, or a new creation.

You will not infer from these remarks that the

change is either physical or mental. The body and its members remain the same; the mind and its faculties remain the same; but they have a new character and new applications; they act from new impulses, and are consecrated to services harmonizing with the claims of religion. As a moral being, however, the transformation is complete. He is a new creature—born from above; he is brought from darkness to light, and from the power of Satan to God; he is quickened from a life of sin to a life of holiness; he now rejoices in conscious pardon and acceptance with God; he is a child of God, and receives the seal of sonship—the Spirit of adoption, whereby he cries, Abba, Father.

3. *It comprehends holiness.*

Holiness is not to be confounded with either justification or regeneration. It includes these, but it implies much more. Whatever this state may be, it is comprehended in the word righteousness. "Without holiness," says the great apostle, "no man shall see the Lord." The Psalmist says, "I shall behold thy face in righteousness." And those who stand in the presence of God are said to be clad in robes of white, "which are the righteousness of the saints." "What," says that eminent divine, Mr. Wesley, "what is that holiness which is the only qualification for glory? In Christ Jesus," he continues, "neither circumcision availeth any thing nor uncircumcision, but faith which worketh by love. It is the keeping the commands of God, particularly these: Thou shalt love the Lord thy God with all thy heart; and thy neighbor as thyself. In a word, holiness is the having the mind that was in Christ, and the walking as he walked." In some notes of difference between himself and the Moravian brethren, he says, "Scripture holiness is the image of God; the mind which was in Christ; the love of God and man, lowliness, gentleness, temperance, patience, chastity." In regard to these views, he says, "Such has been my judgment for threescore years, without any material alteration." Holiness does not seem to differ from regeneration, except in degree. It has its beginning in this state, and all its elements are found in this department of Christian experience. Regeneration is *initial* holiness; to it belong the fruits of the Spirit—power over sin, victory over the world, with every other quality and affection that marks the higher state; only they are immature. Their development and perfection constitute the holiness that qualifies for heaven.

In this state we enjoy a full restoration to the lost image of God. I say lost, for it is now defaced and broken. Sin has not only marred its beauty, but destroyed its existence. The reproduction of that image constitutes us holy. The lineaments appear in the new-born soul; in holiness they are seen in stronger relief, and shine with a heavenly luster. We then, in the highest sense, "put on the new man, which, after God, is renewed in righteousness and true holiness;" "we are made partakers of the divine nature." This, too, first obtains in our renewal; but its fuller experience belongs to the department of Christian holiness. We then enter into fellowship with the divine nature; we are "one with Christ, even as he is one with the Father," and "his blood cleanseth us from all sin." We enjoy the love of God—a love made perfect, "casting out all fear that hath torment." God is now the object of a pure and supreme love. It does not, however, exclude a proper regard for worldly interests or worldly pursuits; it is not inconsistent with a glowing love for friends or home; but its sovereign preference is given to God. It chooses him as its best and highest good, and embraces him with all the energy of a superior and sanctified affection. "Whom have I in heaven but *thee!* and there is none upon earth that I desire beside thee." The soul is now "an habitation of God through the Spirit;" "For he that dwelleth in love dwelleth in God, and God in him." We enjoy perfect resignation to the Divine will. I do not mean that we shall have no will of our own, but we shall fully and cheerfully resign our will to God, to do, to be, or to suffer what he appoints. The Savior in the garden, when he shrunk from the bitter cup, furnishes our example: "Not *my* will but *thine* be done, O heavenly Father!" In this happy frame of mind, we

> "Leave to his sovereign sway
> To choose and to command."

"We walk by faith and not by sight;" "We rejoice evermore, pray without ceasing, and in every thing give thanks." O, blest experience! O, divine estate! when shall we know all thy hights and depths of love? O, thou who hast said, "Be ye holy, for I am holy,"

> "Hallow thy great and glorious name,
> And perfect holiness in *me!*"

And now, as an object of pursuit, how noble and elevating is this righteousness! How trifling is every earthly interest in comparison with this! To be delivered from the grossness and impurity of our nature—to be renewed after the image of God—to be raised to converse and companionship with Christ—to participate in the raptures of divine love: these are objects worthy of our immortal nature and our eternal destiny.

II. LET US NOW CONSIDER THE FEELINGS WITH WHICH WE ARE TO REGARD THE RIGHTEOUSNESS OF THE TEXT.

"Blessed are they which do *hunger* and *thirst* after righteousness." This is a very familiar, but a very expressive figure of speech. Hunger and thirst are the strongest of our bodily appetites; no wants are so keen, and none so imperatively demand supply as these. They occur daily, and when long-continued produce indescribable distress and suffering. These appetites are here intended to represent strong and ardent desire; and no language could more fully indicate the feelings with which we should regard the blessings of salvation. As a man, hungry and faint, traversing a lonely waste, under a burning sun, longs for food, and pants for the cooling water brook, so ardently are we to desire the righteousness of God.

But this phrase describes a character. This, perhaps, was the specific intention; and the description is so graphic, that we see at a glance both the character of the recipient and the terms of receiving. Several things enter into this character.

1. *A consciousness of want.*

Hunger and thirst arise from this source alone, and are felt in all their painfulness only by the famishing. All, therefore who feel the cravings of this spiritual appetite realize their sad condition. They see themselves sinful, polluted, and perishing; they feel their need of Christ and the salvation he offers them; and without this the promise of Christ would be no promise—the blessing he pronounces no blessing; for they alone who feel their wants can value them. What is a physician to them that are whole? or a refuge to them that are safe? Bread is a blessing to the hungry, and water a priceless boon to the thirsty, but to others the offer of bread is a mockery, and the cooling stream rolls uninvitingly by.

When Israel wandered in the desert, "hungry and thirsty, their soul fainted within them." But their condition was less desperate than ours. Our *souls* are in want—want which no created good can supply. Sin is a fearful evil; our whole nature is in ruins under its desolating power, and it is every moment preparing for us a deeper and a darker destruction, where the light of hope will never shine and the hand of mercy never relieve; and whether we feel it or not we *need* pardon! O, how *much* we need it! But sin pollutes; it has entered our hearts and made them like the prophet's chamber of imagery—a "dark storehouse of every abomination." Where sin enters it abides; so dreadful is its nature that to become its victim for one moment is, if left to ourselves, to remain its victim forever. Among all the millions of our race, there is not one who can say, "I have made my heart clean, I am pure from my sin." We need, then, the renewing grace of God; we need the cleansing blood of Christ, without which we are not only guilty, but absolutely lost and undone forever. How many are there who have no realizing sense of their sad estate, and no desire of relief! They feel not their wants, and seem to love their very pollution and wretchedness; but there are those, thank God! who *realize* their condition; they feel a burden upon their hearts, and cry for deliverance; "they hunger and thirst after righteousness."

2. *Intense desire.*

This results from a discovery of their condition; and the more distressing that condition is felt to be, the more earnest will be the desire of relief. Take the case of a penitent sinner. How painful his convictions, how appalling his sense of danger! No pains of hunger or thirst can represent the agony of his spirit, or his intense desire for the salvation of God. With what abhorrence does he now regard his former pursuits! His affections had been set on the world; he had chosen it as his supreme good; but he now sees its emptiness, and sighs for a better portion. How vain to him is all this wealth, this splendor, this rank, for which the world around is toiling! To know that his sins are pardoned, that he is saved from the hell he fears, that he is now a child of God—every thing beside dwindles into insignificance; and to hear others speak of pardon and proclaim the raptures of divine love, only stimulates his desires, and renders his hunger and thirst more intense.

"I starve, he cries, nor can I bear
The famine in this land,
While servants of my father share
The bounties of his hand."

Take the believer, who has already tasted that the Lord is good. Conscious of remaining corruptions, and enlightened by the Spirit to perceive the privileges yet before him, with what energy of desire does he pant for the "clean heart and the pure spirit!" To know the full salvation of God, to taste all the sweetness of divine love, and enjoy a full conformity to the will of God—these are objects that engross all his wishes, and kindle his desires with an ever-burning flame. "I have opened my mouth and panted," says the Psalmist, "for I longed for thy salvation;" "As the hart panteth after the water brook, so panteth my soul after thee, O God!" O, to be made free from sin—to be delivered from this bondage of corruption! When will the bright morning dawn that shall emancipate my captive soul? How fitly do the glowing words of Charles Wesley express this experience:

"I *thirst* for a life-giving God,
  A God that on Calvary died—
A fountain of water and blood,
  That gushed from Immanuel's side!
I *gasp* for the streams of thy love,
  The spirit of rapture unknown,
And then to redrink it above
  Eternally fresh from thy throne."

Former *experience* adds to the fervency of his desires. He has tasted that the Lord is gracious; he has felt the comforts of pardoning mercy; and the relish of enjoyment adds to the sense of want—he would know more of God. His soul flies with infinite desire from the streams to the fountain, and can only be satisfied when it is filled with all the fullness of God.

3. *Unremitting effort.*

Hunger and thirst prompt to exertion. Superhuman efforts have been put forth to satisfy their cravings; and they who hunger and thirst after righteousness, will exert themselves to secure the object of their desire.

This desire does not end in fruitless wishes. It makes a man look out for relief and exert himself to be saved. Look into the Scriptures: "Strive," says Jesus, "to enter into the strait gate, for many shall seek to enter in and shall not be able;" "Give all diligence to make your calling and election sure;" "Work out your salvation with fear and trembling." True, these efforts do not save us; of themselves they are nothing; but God has connected them with this result, and has promised to crown them with his blessing. And yet how often do men say, I am all weakness, I can do nothing; and with this they sit down without an effort! Deceitful sophistry! was it thus the prodigal regained his father's house and blessing? and of all the redeemed sinners who now live on earth, or sing and shine in heaven, was there ever one thus saved? The desire of which I speak stirs a man; it separates him from the world; it makes him a man of self-denial and prayer; it prompts to diligence in every means of grace. He will now turn from his evil ways; he will mortify his corruptions; he will resist temptation. With an eagerness that nothing can repress he will fly to the word of God, to the throne of grace, and to the sanctuary of the Most High. "O!" he cries, "that I knew *where* I might find him! I would come even to his *seat;* I would order my cause before him; I would fill my mouth with arguments."

Turn now to the Christian. How does this desire affect him? Does it produce ease and indifference?

No. It fills him with spiritual ardor; it prompts him forward in the way of holiness. He feels that it is his privilege to enter into rest, to enjoy the love of Christ, which passeth knowledge, and he seeks for it as for hidden treasure. He *labors* to enter into rest. As he values Christ above every thing else, so he seeks him above every thing else; and nothing grieves him more than the want of zeal and ardor in the pursuit. He seeks with various feelings; sometimes, like the Ethiopian convert, rejoicing; sometimes, like Joseph and Mary, sorrowing; sometimes, like the woman who touched the hem of his garment, trembling; but whether happy or sad, in sickness or health, in joy or sorrow, he is inquiring for the Savior, and will not rest till he finds a full salvation. In his works he looks for him, in his house he draws near to him, in prayer he thirsts for his love. To him the word is precious, because it exhibits his grace; and even afflictions are valuable, because "they yield the peaceable fruits of righteousness." Thus, impelled by strong desire, does he "press toward the mark for the prize of his high calling of God in Christ Jesus." "And, O, my brethren, we desire that every one of you do show the same diligence, to the full assurance of hope unto the end; that ye be not slothful, but followers of them who through faith and patience inherit the promises."

4. *Confiding faith.*

And hence says Christ, "He that *cometh* to me shall never hunger, and he that *believeth* on me shall never thirst." The blessings of salvation are offered only upon this condition. Faith, therefore, must distinguish all who truly hunger and thirst after righteousness. What we ask of God we must ask in faith, "nothing wavering; for he that wavereth, is like a wave of the sea, driven with the wind and tossed. Let not that man think that he shall receive any thing of the Lord." And this faith is not the mere belief of our perishing condition, or a mere persuasion of our need of mercy; but a firm belief that if we seek we shall find, if we ask it shall be given unto us.

Evangelical faith not only believes but trusts. It is *confiding* faith. He who possesses it takes the atonement of Christ as his only plea, and the promises of Christ as his only assurance, and pleads them before the mercy-seat. He rests in them, assured and satisfied that they can not be disregarded, and that his suit can not be in vain.

This faith, then, is not a mere notion, but a principle, and it always produces an application to the Savior. Under its influence I feel all the woes of my perishing condition. I see that he is the appointed, complete, and *willing* Savior; I see that "in him all fullness dwells." I fly to him; I fall at his feet; I cry, "Lord save, or I perish;" "Lord, if thou wilt thou canst make me clean." He smiles and bids me come. I throw myself into his open arms; for now, like Paul, I see that "he loved me and gave himself for me." Let us now turn to consider,

III. The interesting promise of the Savior: "Blessed are they which do hunger and thirst after righteousness: *for they shall be filled.*"

How appropriate is this promise, and how precisely adapted to their condition! Gold and jewels can not allay the pains of hunger or quench the fires of thirst. They have no adaptation to these appetites. And so, if you could transmute every created atom into gold, and lay it at the feet of him who truly feels his lost estate, he would turn from it with disgust and loathing. The salvation of God alone can fill the emptiness of the heart and satisfy the cravings of the immortal soul.

1. *They shall be filled.*

That is, they shall find what they seek. They shall obtain what they so ardently pant for. Do they desire the renewal of their hearts? It shall be granted. Though now bowed down under a load of guilt—though now perishing in a barren waste—though now fainting with desire to taste the sweets of redeeming love, they shall yet realize the truth of this precious promise. God, blessed be his name! never inspired a wish or a prayer he did not intend to gratify. He does not mock the wants of penitence by an unmeaning parade of promise; but holds himself in readiness to grant all that abject want can crave or suppliant misery demand. That load of guilt shall be rolled away, and those longing desires shall be fully gratified; for the very heavens shall drop down manna, and "the skies shall pour down righteousness." Or do they desire the full salvation of God; "all the blessings of the new covenant; all the graces of Messiah's kingdom?" These, too, shall be granted; for the promise comprehends all that can possibly enter into Christian experience, from the first sigh of penitence till the redeemed spirit takes its place among the glorified in heaven. Having tasted the joys of pardon and the comforts of adopting love, whatever else they may hunger for, whatever of conformity to the Divine will, of the gifts and fruits of the Holy Spirit, of the cleansing blood of Christ, of the perfect love of God, why, "blessed are they, for they shall be filled." And then, after all this, God is "able to do exceeding abundantly above all that they can ask or think."

2. *For this result God has made an infinite provision.*

This provision is developed in the Gospel. Its grand design was to prepare and spread out a "great feast for all people," and then to circulate far and wide the generous invitation, "Come, for all things are now ready." Every demand of our nature has been contemplated, and every necessity provided for. Are we guilty? Here is pardon. Are we dead in sins? Here is life. Are we defiled? Here is an open, ever-flowing fountain to wash away our sins. Here is light for our darkness, strength for our weakness, renovation for the heart, and peace for the conscience. However large your desires, however ardent your thirstings after righteousness, however inadequate all other supplies, here is "enough for all, for each, for evermore." "My God shall supply all your need;" "the blood of Christ cleanseth from all sin, and he is faithful and just to cleanse you from all unrighteousness." Come, then, ye weary and heavy laden; come ye that pant for the clean heart and the pure spirit; come and "eat ye that which is good, and let your soul delight itself in fatness."

3. *This is a satisfying portion.*

The idea is that of *perfect* satisfaction. Man has hopes and wishes that nothing earthly can realize. The world presents its wealth, its pleasures, its honors. They are sought and gained; but happiness, like a brilliant phantom, eludes the grasp and is yet far in the future. Nothing below the skies can fill the immortal mind or confer lasting enjoyment. In every disappointment men realize vexation, and in every success vanity. And yet we have seen men in the lowest walks of life, unlettered, poor, afflicted, and even despised by the purse-proud worldling, possess an elevation of soul and a perfection of bliss to which the throned monarch is a stranger. Whence is this? Let us hear the Savior: "I am the bread of life; he that cometh to me shall never hunger, and he that believeth on me shall never thirst. Whosoever drinketh of this water that I shall give him shall never thirst: but the water that I shall give him, shall be in him a well of water springing up unto everlasting life." These assurances disclose the true secret of happiness; and they who have been refreshed at this fountain enjoy what they never did before—satisfaction. Once they sought earthly good, and realized only bitter disappointment. But having now tasted the sweets of heavenly love, they cry, "Lord, evermore give us this bread." O what a contrast is there between them and others! The mirthful and gay may boast of their pleasures; but no pleasure, no delight can compare with that which flows from an experience of the salvation of God. It is not, however, a satisfaction which destroys the spiritual appetite. It is continued, even increased. But though continued it is relieved, and though increased there is still an adequate supply. Still infinite provisions remain for their indulgence and enjoyment. And O with what fervent but rapturous desire do they exclaim,

"My earth thou waterest from on high,
But make it all a pool;
Spring up, O well, I ever cry;
Spring up within my soul!"

But though he hungers and thirsts, it is not in vain. He knows where to go for blessings, and is never disappointed in his applications. He has found in God a permanent good, and, "fixed on that blissful center," he rests with inexpressible pleasure and delight. For the complete fulfillment of the promise he looks to the paradise of God, where he shall hunger no more, neither thirst any more; but where the Lamb that is in the midst of the throne shall *feed* them, and lead them to fountains of *living water*, and God shall wipe all tears from their eyes. In reviewing this subject we see

1. *In what our true interest consists.*

And this is simply in the attainment of righteousness, the renewal of our hearts, and their conformity to the image and will of God. These blessings harmonize with our spiritual nature; they deliver us from the terrible evils of sin; they elevate us to friendship and communion with the Redeemer, and the everlasting fruition of God in heaven. We are destined to an eternal state; and long after the sun shall have burned out his fires, and the last star shall have ceased to twinkle in the heavens, the soul shall live in all the vigor of its immortality. Whatever promotes our holiness and happiness in that world must be regarded as our chief good, and every thing else is of trifling importance. How wearisome and fruitless are the pursuits of the present life! What is wealth, or fame, or human applause? "Mere useless sounds, and empty as the bubbles of the deep." In the possession of them all men have died in horrible remorse, and sunk to the perdition of hell. O that you could feel the vanity of all creature good! O that you could realize the supreme importance of religion! How many have I seen cheated of their hopes and their salvation by the *neglect* of religion! They awoke too late, and perished the victims of their own folly. Will you perversely fall into the same snare? With open eyes will you rush upon the same terrible and hopeless ruin? No, I beseech you, no. O thou immortal soul, believe me, but *one* thing is needful! Choose that good part, and when heaven and earth have passed away this shall remain to cheer and bless you forever.

2. *We see, too, with what earnestness and relish you should seek your salvation.*

If you have ever felt or can imagine the anguish of hunger and thirst, you may form an idea of the feelings with which you are to seek the salvation of God. With the same keen sense of want; with the same restless and craving appetite with which the famishing cry for food, you are to seek the salvation of your soul. The formal and the worldly will call this enthusiasm and rant; but remember, religion is more than formality, and your sinful condition and the commands of Jehovah are awful realities. The kingdom of God is not in word, but in power. You are to hunger and thirst. Two things demand of you all this fervor of desire and all this energy of pursuit—the nature of the blessings and your own necessities. They are the richest and the best that God can bestow. No present of gold or silver; no earthly crown or kingdom, however splendid, can compare with them. They are durable riches and righteousness, for which some, who have known them best, have surrendered all of earth and joyfully laid down their lives. And then your necessities. You are a fallen, sinful, ruined man. You stand upon the very threshold of eternity. Over your head hangs the doom of death, and at your feet yawns the devouring jaws of hell. And is there no reason here why you should long with infinite desire to be saved from sin? O man, you are *perishing*—perishing *forever!* Will you, can you rest amid such appalling dangers?

Talk not of heartless desires and feeble efforts when your soul is sinking into hell. Infinite desires and the mightiest efforts alone befit such a condition. Were all the powers of your immortal nature transformed into desire, that desire would fall infinitely below the necessities of your case. I repeat, you are perishing, O sinner, and all your soul should awake to the pursuit of that salvation purchased for you by the blood of Christ. O careless man, is your soul safe? Has its condition ever occupied your thoughts or your anxieties? You have asked a thousand times, What shall I eat, and what shall I drink? But have you ever asked, *What must I do to be saved?* If not, it needs no voice from heaven to tell you that you are lost. Away with indifference. Be in earnest. Eternal interests are at stake, and your soul is trembling on the very brink of ruin.

3. *And, finally, we see the encouragement of all who seek the salvation of God.*

No matter who, no matter where, whether rich or poor, bond or free, wise or ignorant, in civilized or savage lands, to each and to all who hunger and thirst after righteousness, the promise is full and sure—they shall be filled. Are you seeking the knowledge of salvation? Here is your encouragement; you can not seek in vain. "If any man thirst, let him come unto me and drink." He who uttered these words has also said, "I *will give* unto him that is athirst of the fountain of the water of life freely." Come, then, to him. Believe his promise and he will give thee "to eat of the fatness of his house, and make thee to drink of the river of his pleasure."

Or dost thou desire more? Wouldst thou go on to perfection? Dost thou hunger and thirst for a full salvation? Blessed art thou, for thou shalt be filled. Be strong in faith. Stagger not at the promise through unbelief. Is any thing too hard for the Lord? Believe the promise and expect its fulfillment. Wait in all the means of his appointment, and when fainting with delay, let the language of the Psalmist reassure thy sinking hopes: "I *shall* behold thy face in righteousness; I shall be *satisfied* when I wake in thy likeness."

LECTURE VI.

FIFTH BEATITUDE.

"Blessed are the merciful: for they shall obtain mercy." MATTHEW v, 7.

CHRISTIANITY is a system which requires us to consult the happiness of others, as well as our own. In this it differs from all merely-human systems, and exhibits one of its many proofs that it came from God. Among others, they have this one mark of their earthly origin—they pander to selfishness. They are, therefore, always agreeable to the sinful heart, and meet with favor when every thing else may be rejected.

Under the sway of selfishness, a vice common to all fallen beings, we look to our individual profit. In the expressive language of St. Paul, "We live to ourselves;" we seek to promote our own elevation and happiness; or, if we glance beyond the narrow circle of self, it is because our interests are interwoven with others', and can only be secured in connection with theirs. Selfishness is a deadly evil, and beyond all others destructive of good. Winter does not more certainly freeze the flowing streams, than selfishness the kindly sympathies of the soul. Death does not more certainly kill the body, than does this hateful vice that divine charity which "suffereth long and is kind." Like mildew it blights, like a canker it corrodes. It has no heart to feel, no eye to weep, no hand to help. These are alone possessed by Mercy, but she dwells not in the selfish heart; her element is not there; she has sought a home in purer bosoms, or fled to her native skies. Think of a world, if you can without a shudder, where selfishness alone reigns—a world without a brother or a friend; without one tender heart, or one emotion of pity, or one hand stretched forth in relief of suffering man; full of tigers in human shape, roaming for prey and thirsting for blood. Such a world would be hell, and such a hell would this world be, without the light and influences of Christianity.

The destruction of the selfish principle is one of the great aims of the Christian religion. Its entire structure is adapted to this end, and it is only necessary to bring the heart under its divine sway, in order to realize this blissful result. The spirit of benevolence, so often and so fully brought to view in the Gospel, stands in direct opposition to it; and that particular mode of goodness, called mercy, is every-where enjoined upon men as essential to their perfection in virtue, and their final acceptance with God. Sometimes it is enjoined by direct command; sometimes it is encouraged by promise; then, again, it is displayed in character, and moves before us as an angel of light, while a Savior's voice pronounces, "Blessed are the merciful: for they shall obtain mercy."

Here we shall pause for a moment to inquire into the nature of Christian mercy, or that principle which actuates the merciful. The word is said to be of classic origin, being derived from the Latin word *misericordia*, and literally signifies pain of heart, produced by the sight of misery. It implies that benevolence, or tenderness of heart, which disposes a person to overlook injuries, or to treat a person better than he deserves; it induces long-suffering and forgiveness; it tempers justice and softens the rigor of punishment; it implies pity and compassion, and prompts the heart to relieve distress and suffering. Mercy is a distinguishing attribute of God. "The Lord is long-suffering, and of great mercy; he is merciful and gracious." And under no circumstances do we so much resemble him, as in the exercise of this divine principle. Christian mercy, which our Savior here so beautifully commends, is a supernatural principle; God is its source, and whether it exists in men or angels, it is derived from him. "The capacity," says one, "every human being possesses;" but a new heart is indispensable to its growth and expansion; there alone it finds congenial soil, and there alone it flourishes. The effect of sin is always to harden the heart and blunt its sensibilities; but in our renewal God "takes the stony out of our heart and gives us a heart of flesh." It is now tender and sensitive; it is touched with sympathy; it hears the cry of distress; it melts at human woe. There may be in many hearts much of generous and kindly feeling, but Christian mercy only flows from a heart softened by the influences of the Spirit. It is a fruit of the Spirit, and is one of the bright offspring of that wisdom which cometh down from above. Let us now,

I. Trace the practical manifestations of this principle.

This will embody the quality and display the

character in its active form. I repeat, its *practical* manifestations; for it is a vigorous and working principle. It does not lie dormant or slumbering in the heart, nor does it merely weep and sigh; but it comes forth with a strong arm and ready hand in deeds of kindness and mercy. "It deviseth liberal things," and is fruitful in expedients of relief. There is, indeed, much in the world that passes under the name of pity and tenderness. We often hear it said, I pity that man, I am sorry for his misfortunes; and the superficial observer commends such a one as a kind-hearted and merciful man. But is this Christian mercy? No more than the fitful gleams of sunshine in winter are the warming, fertilizing beams of spring, which cheer the earth and bring forth the flowers and fruits of summer. Christian mercy is indeed a sensitive principle, but its chief profession is not in word but in *deed*. The head deviseth plans of mercy; the tongue pleads the cause of mercy, and the hands minister to the objects of mercy.

1. *Then this principle exhibits itself in kindness to inferior animals.*

God, in the plentitude of his goodness, has been pleased to call into being innumerable orders, lower in the scale of creation than man. These are variously endowed with sense and motion, from the almost inanimate shell-fish, up to that which, in organic perfection, ranks next to man. These are all his creatures; he gave them existence, and has opened sources of enjoyment to them agreeable to their nature. As they form a part of his wide-spread family, his kind providence is over them to protect their lives, and satisfy their wants. The Scriptures speak expressly upon this subject. "Doth God," says St. Paul, "care for oxen?" And the fact that he is solicitous for their welfare, is shown by framing an express law in their behalf: "Thou shalt not muzzle the ox that treadeth out the corn;" "Not a sparrow," says our blessed Lord, "falleth to the ground without the notice of your heavenly Father." The Psalmist, in celebrating the divine mercy, says, "He giveth to the beast his food, and to the young ravens which cry;" "The eyes of all wait upon thee, and thou givest them their meat in due season. Thou openest thine hand and satisfiest the desire of every living thing." Such, then, are the displays of Divine regard to the lower orders of creation. Will not the merciful seek to imitate these beautiful manifestations?

"A righteous man," says an inspired proverb, "regardeth the life of his beast; but the tender mercies of the wicked are cruel." A man who can wantonly inflict pain and suffering upon a brute, or even a worm, is an unfeeling monster, and a righteous God will not hold him guiltless. Man himself has scarcely a keener sense of wrong and pain than they. "The lioness robbed of her whelps, causes the wilderness to ring with the story of her wrongs; and the bird, whose little household has been stolen by the cruel boy, saddens the grove with melodies of deepest sorrow." But how deep, often, are the sufferings which the poor dumb animal can not tell, and against which it can offer no remonstrance! Though it utter no cry, its anguish is not the less real.

"The poor beetle that we tread upon,
In corporal suffering, feels a pang as great
As when a giant dies."

But there is an eloquence in its silence, an eloquence that pleads not in vain, in the ears of Him who regardeth the meanest of his works.

But has not God "given all things into our hand? All sheep and oxen; yea, and the beasts of the field, the fowl of the air, and the fish of the sea?" He has, but not for purposes of cruelty, not even for abuse. We have a right to use them in a way harmonizing with the Divine intention. We may even take their lives, when necessary, to sustain our own. But he has never licensed the indiscriminate and wholesale slaughter of beasts, birds, and fishes, that every-where prevails, or granted permission to inflict needless pain, by cruel goads or cutting whips. And the man who, in sport or passion, overtaxes their strength, maims them by savage blows, or subjects them to unnecessary hardship, gives evidence of a brutal nature and a wicked heart.

"The merciful man regardeth the life of his beast." He views them as the creatures of God, sharing with himself the attentions of a benignant Providence; he uses them without abuse; he provides for their wants, and by tender offices seeks to mitigate their sufferings; and in doing this imitates the benevolent Father of all, whose "tender mercies are over all his works."

2. *It displays itself in sympathy and aid toward the afflicted and suffering of mankind.*

All men suffer; it is the universal consequence of sin; not an exception has been known in the history of our world. "If a man live many days, and rejoice in them all, yet let him remember the days of darkness, for they shall be many." The sufferings of men arise from various causes; sometimes from poverty. The poor have existed in all ages, and they "shall never cease out of the land." Poverty is sometimes, perhaps, a heritage from God, and arises out of his all-wise appointment; but it is more frequently the result of imprudence and wickedness. Multitudes are poor in spite of the rich and ever-flowing bounties of Providence. Thrift and industry would secure the necessaries, if not the luxuries of life; but idleness and sottish waste doom them to poverty. Many, like the prodigal, spend the earnings of a parent's labor in sumptuous fare, in gay apparel, and splendid entertainments, and finally sink into obscurity and want. *Vice* brings poverty, and none sooner or more certainly than intemperance. Upon the inebriate "want cometh as an armed man." Vainly may he struggle against its encroachments—come it will, and, like an unfeeling tyrant, turn him out of his pleasant home, strip off his costly robes, and send him forth upon the world, in rags and wretchedness.

Abject poverty, from whatever cause, is a sore evil. To feel the agonizing pains of hunger—to shiver in scanty raiment before the wintery storm—to dwell amid the gloom of a cheerless and squalid home, unlit by a ray of comfort, is a sad inheritance, and the only one possessed by thousands in the world. Bodily affliction is a source of suffering. Go forth into the world; walk the streets and lanes of a populous city; enter the damp basement, or the wind-rent garret: there upon a pallet of straw lies the child of sorrow, languishing in pain. The eye has lost its fire—the cheek its bloom—the limbs their wonted strength. Earthly resources have long since perished. Wasting under the hand of disease, he gradually sinks under accumulating woes, till death kindly puts a period to his sufferings. Many suffer under sore bereavements—the wife, widowed of her husband, pines in sadness and solitude; her earthly support gone, her best and truest friend carried to the grave, and she left to brave the storms of life alone; the orphan bewailing, with bitter tears, the loss of parents, and now cast upon an unfeeling world, with no mother's heart to sympathize, and no father's hand to protect. In *such* a world, so full of sad reverses; where sorrow, like a stormy sea, rolls its mountain waves; where there are so many broken and bleeding hearts, how ample is the field of Christian benevolence! Here Mercy may unburden her full heart, and dispense the bounties of her liberal hand. Amid these scenes of human woe, Christian mercy displays itself in heart-felt sympathy. "Rejoice with them that do rejoice; and weep with them that weep," is one of the beautiful precepts of religion. So feels the true Christian, as, in imitation of Jesus, he goes "about doing good;" but it is not only thus, or even by soothing words, that he meets the various forms of suffering—"he visits the widow and fatherless in their affliction, drawing out his soul to the hungry, and satisfying the poor with bread." A touching and beautiful illustration of his benevolent career occurs in the history of Job, a man not more remarkable for his sufferings than for his tenderness of heart. Appealing to heaven for the rectitude of his conduct, he says, "I delivered the poor that cried, the fatherless, and him that had none to help him. The blessing of him that was ready to perish came upon me; and I caused the widow's heart to sing for joy. I was eyes to the blind, and feet was I to the lame. I was a father to the poor: and the cause which I knew not I searched out." Such a man was John Howard, the great philanthropist. The relief of human suffering was his profession and employment; for this he left the abodes of wealth and the pleasures of home; he traveled by sea and land; he journeyed over the world; he entered the infected hospital, the damp and filthy dungeon; he went down to the lowest point of human degradation and sorrow; and by labors in which he never wearied, and to which he at last fell a victim, sought to assuage the griefs and mitigate the woes of his brother man. Well might such a man be called an angel of mercy; for he seems to have descended from a heavenly sphere—sent awhile below to bless and brighten our sin-cursed world.

Such a disposition is essential to Christian character. And to fancy that heaven will regard a sanctimonious face, and long prayers, where there is a pitiless and illiberal heart, is a deep and strong delusion. "Whoso hath this world's good, and seeth his brother have need, and shutteth up his bowels of compassion from him, how dwelleth the love of God in him?"

3. *It displays itself in efforts to alleviate the spiritual miseries of our fellow-men.*

This ranks among its noblest exercises. Temporal and spiritual miseries are very dissimilar things; the one has to do with the body, the other with the soul: that relates only to the present world, this to both the present and the future. "There is a spirit in man;" that spirit has fallen from its allegiance to God, and has become sinful and corrupt. This is the condition of the whole race; among all the millions of mankind, there is not one exception. Men of every clime and country, of every color and condition, from the degraded Caffre to the accomplished European, are sinners. The whole *world* lieth in wickedness; all have sinned and come short of the glory of God. In this condition men are *perishing;* the *world* is perishing, and sinking into the gulf of perdition. "Even while we are reflecting upon it," says the eloquent Reed, "many have reached the limit of probation, and are precipitated from a life of sin to a state of punishment, and shriek to find themselves forever lost!" Such is our world; a vast prison-house, full of guilty rebels, where men by millions sin, and by millions perish! O, who can think of it without deep emotion? If we pity the suffering body, how should we feel when we look upon a *dying soul?* If the spirit of Paul was stirred when he beheld a single city given to idolatry, what feelings should possess us when we see a *world* wandering from God, and groaning under the bondage of sin and Satan? Where is the heart that can fully appreciate such a condition? Where are the tears fit to be wept over such a scene?

"Mercy to the soul," says one, "is the soul of

mercy." The most illustrious display which our world has ever witnessed, was in the life and conduct of the Son of God. His was a heart of infinite mercy; it lived and moved embodied in Jesus of Nazareth. All that he did to alleviate our physical sufferings, affords but a feeble type of what he did to snatch the immortal soul from ruin. "What," said he, "shall it profit a man if he gain the whole world and lose his own soul; or, what shall a man give in exchange for his soul?" He alone could estimate its true value; he alone knew its awful perils. And to save that priceless immortal spirit from endless torments, he humbled himself from the shining thrones of heaven, to the condition of a poor, despised, and persecuted man, and finally poured out his precious blood upon the cross, that he might open a way of salvation from sin to holiness, and from earth to heaven.

Now, when this divine principle actuates the human heart, it aims at the same sublime result—the salvation of the soul from sin and its terrible consequences in a future world. Like the blessed Jesus, when he wept over the guilt and ruin of Jerusalem, it sympathizes with the condition of sinners, and bewails their impending doom; it beholds them exposed to hell, and longs to rescue them from its everlasting flames.

Acting under the promptings of mercy, the Christian makes direct personal efforts for the salvation of men. He instructs the ignorant; he exhorts the erring; he warns the unruly. Having himself been made a partaker of salvation, he seeks to bestow it upon others. All that he says or does is under the control of a peculiar temper; the Scriptures beautifully call it the "meekness of wisdom." Its power you will see in the following incident: "When I was yet young and thoughtless," says an eminent minister, "a pious man addressed me about my salvation. I was angry; my heart rose in bitterness against him; I reproached him; I talked, indeed, like a madman, while my conscience was grinding me like a millstone. He bore it all with meekness, perfectly unmoved. If he had only given one retort, shown one angry feeling, it would have relieved me. His Christian kindness was too much for me; I went into the forest smarting from my wounds; I fell under what he had said to me, and went and asked his pardon." This was the meekness of wisdom. He seeks their salvation by prayer. O, with what intense desire does he wrestle in supplication, for the outpouring of the Spirit and the rescue of sinners from the wrath to come!—and fervent prayer availeth much. Efforts in conjunction with *others* distinguish the merciful; he is one in heart and feeling with every benevolent enterprise; he does not stop to ask, Who originated the scheme? Will it bring honor to me or my party? No, he soars above such unworthy views. It is enough that it will bless a guilty world, and he hastens to give it his sympathy and co-operation. Among other schemes, the three following especially engage his ardent and effective co-operation. 1. The *Sabbath school cause.* No merely-human expedient stands more intimately related to the work of man's salvation. The religious instruction of the young, the proper training of the moral faculties, and the formation of moral and virtuous habits, must ever be regarded as promotive both of the purity and happiness of the race. Nothing would go further to redeem the world, in the next generation, from the slavery of ignorance and vice, than the success of its simple but sublime intentions. How many young minds now in darkness would then kindle into intelligence under the light of truth! How many young hearts would learn to glow with the hopes and the happiness of religion! How many millions now doomed to a life of crime and an end of infamy, would then be rescued from the destroyer, and raised to the dignity and companionship of angels! 2. The *Bible cause.* A single purpose directs and animates the efforts of this association: that purpose is to place the Bible in the hands of every man, that he may read in his own tongue the wonderful works of God. Mercy in man, flowing out to a sinful brother man, can impart no higher, holier gift than this. "It is more precious than rubies, and all the things thou canst desire are not to be compared to it." 3. The *missionary cause.* This he regards as one of the first agencies in the salvation of the world. As its object is to preach the Gospel to every creature—a Gospel which contains the only remedy for sin and sorrow; and as he himself is a witness of its efficacy, it becomes his first desire to convey to the world that word of life which invites all to be saved, and in the reception of which he beholds paradise restored, and this world of guilt and woe changed into a heaven of purity and joy. In such efforts as these we behold the brightest displays of Christian mercy.

4. *This principle exhibits itself in the exercise of lenity to the unfortunate, under pecuniary embarrassment.*

This arises from various causes, and occasionally befalls the best of men. Providential afflictions, convulsions in the commercial world, inattention or want of capacity in business, are among the most common causes of pecuniary trouble. How often do men, under these circumstances, and with the spirit of a "Shylock," pursue the unfortunate debtor! Like a famished wolf, they track and hunt him down, and then, without pity or remorse, strip him of all his goods, and consign his helpless family to beggary. Thus have I seen a professing Christian treat a debtor, and that debtor a gray-haired man, a man of misfortune and a Christian brother, and I thought,

> "What has the gray-haired prisoner done?
> Has murder stained his hands with gore?
> Not so; his crime's a fouler one—
> *God made the old man poor!*
> For this he shares a felon's cell,
> The fittest earthly type of hell."

I said a professing Christian; but what a mockery! Is it possible that such a man can fancy himself a Christian, when he has not the compassions of a heathen? or imagine for a moment that any one can be deceived by such bold and black hypocrisy as this? Let every such merciless and vindictive creditor remember, that "whoso stoppeth his ears at the cry of the poor, he also shall cry himself, but will not be heard."

In a pecuniary sense, the exercise of mercy is better than exacting oppression. It will inspire confidence, and stimulate to exertion, while a contrary course will only mortify and crush the spirit already broken by misfortune, thus preventing the very result it thought to secure. A Christian creditor will not pursue this course; he will exercise mercy toward the unfortunate. Though the law may favor him; though in sheer justice he might strip his debtor of every farthing, yet he will not take advantage of his necessities, or grind him down by cruel exactions. He will wait; he will exercise forbearance, and, by sympathy and kindness, will seek to inspire hope, and excite to honest and persevering effort. I do not at all hesitate to say, that such a course would do more to secure the payment of debts, than legislative enactments, or the pains and penalties of law. I do not say that we are to submit to fraud, that we are not to seek and maintain our rights, or that we are quietly to yield to the plunderings of men, who deal only in *promises to pay;* but I do say that we are to exercise mercy to the unfortunate, and that, when compelled to invoke the strong arm of law, and the entire advantage is ours, we are not to trample down the rights of others to secure our own. Such was the conduct of the merciless creditor in the parable of the Savior. Though he himself had been forgiven a debt of ten thousand talents, yet he took his fellow-servant by the throat, saying, "Pay me that thou owest." And his fellow-servant fell at his feet, and besought him, saying, "Have patience with me and I will pay thee all; yet he would not, but cast him into prison till he should pay the debt." How justly was his Lord wroth, who, in turn, "delivered *him* to the tormentors, till he should pay all that was due!" Thus, we are taught, shall God treat the harsh and cruel; "for he shall have judgment without mercy, that hath showed no mercy."

5. *Mercy displays itself in acts of forbearance and charity toward our enemies.*

Mercy, in this case, assumes much the character of Christian meekness, of which I have already spoken. But I wish here, especially, to direct your attention to the exercise of this principle, when tempted to resent affronts and revenge injuries. Under such circumstances, a Christian will not give way to the violence of passion, or hasten to take vengeance upon an enemy. Though "pierced to the soul by the venomed shaft of wrong," he will not harbor even the thought of revenge. The beautiful example of the Savior has taught him a different lesson; and he will, therefore, pity his foe, and leave it to a higher power to redress his wrongs; and in doing this, displays a magnanimity of soul unknown to the malicious and revengeful.

Perhaps the most fiend-like passion that ever ruled the heart is revenge. Certainly, men never so much resemble demons as when under its influence. "It is cruel as the grave—the coals thereof are coals of fire." The crimes to which it has prompted men make the very blood run chill—crimes that have branded them with infamy through life, or brought them to a felon's death upon the gallows. This is the devil that rules the bosom of the slanderer, the assassin, the duelist. Upon the crime of dueling allow me to pause for a moment—a crime at once the most absurd and atrocious of which men have ever been guilty. Who, in the hour of calm reflection, can regard it in a different light? And yet these men profess to be governed by a "high sense of honor." But where is the honor? It is here: he has stood up, like a simpleton, to be shot at by another of equal intelligence, or he has "killed his man," and sent a soul, itself reeking with the blood of murder, into the presence of God. And now he is a man of honor! *No*, he is a murderer, whether blood is spilt or not, and the blood of murder is on his hands and heart. Nor are they less guilty who "second" such cold-hearted and infernal butchery. Men of honor! Never was there a more infamous abuse of language. But the consequences—

"Revenge at first, though sweet,
Bitter erelong back on itself recoils."

These men, I know, seem to be calm and even happy; but remorse, with vulture beak and tiger claws, preys upon their hearts. The end of an American duelist is thus narrated by an eminent lawyer: "He was gay, and seemed to have forgotten the murder; but he never slept without a light in his room, and in three years after the event sunk into a drunkard's grave. But his death!—we were present, and may we never witness such another! The subject so long unmentioned was at last broken by himself. With glaring eyes he exclaimed, 'I could not help it!' We tried to turn his thoughts to another subject, but in vain. 'I could not help it, could I?' he exclaimed. Then he cried out wildly, 'It will not do; I murdered him; I see him now. I have seen him, as he lay dead upon the field, ever since I slew him. My God! my God!' and with a shriek, such as I never heard a mortal utter, he died."

In contrast with the ferocious spirit of revenge, mark the sublime lessons of the Christian religion in relation to the treatment of enemies: "Dearly beloved, avenge not yourselves, but rather give place unto wrath: for it is written, Vengeance is mine; I will repay, saith the Lord." "*Love* your enemies," says its divine author, "and do good, and lend, hoping for nothing again; and your reward shall be great. . . . Be ye therefore merciful, as your Father also is merciful." Let us now

II. Reflect upon the manner in which God will reward and honor this character: "Blessed are the merciful: for *they shall obtain mercy*."

The same sentiment is expressed often in the Scriptures. "Whosoever," says Jesus, "shall give a cup of cold water only unto one of these little ones, *in the name of a disciple*, shall not lose his reward." That is, when mercy is shown to its proper objects, in obedience to the command of God, and with the desire that he should be honored, he will regard it as done to himself, and will reward us accordingly. This harmonizes both with the principles and proceedings of the Divine government. "With the merciful," says the Psalmist, "thou wilt show thyself merciful, and with the froward thou wilt show thyself froward." "They shall obtain mercy." This is one of God's most interesting promises. Mercy is our first and greatest want; and no thought can be more terrible than that God should deal with us in justice unmixed with mercy. Our race would perish; the *best* even would fall by a righteous judgment. But we are here assured of mercy, if we extend it toward our fellow-men. God will then compassionate our miseries, relieve our distresses, and forgive our great and manifold sins. This promise comprehends, among others, the following advantages:

1. *The exercise of mercy makes us like the Father of mercies.*

God is indeed such; in nothing does he delight more than its exercise. Man may dismiss compassion from his heart, but God never will.

> "The greatest attribute of heaven is mercy,
> And 'tis the crown of justice and the glory,
> Where it may crush with right, to save with pity."

To us guilty sinners God has shown infinite mercy. The gift of his Son—his death upon the cross—his willingness to pardon, and the mission of his Spirit, sent to renew and sanctify our hearts, are all the outflowings of free and unmerited mercy. Now, in the exercise of mercy, we resemble him; and in nothing else can we approach so near the perfection and bliss of God himself.

2. *This promise secures an interest in the merciful arrangements of Providence.*

God is both a wise and benevolent sovereign, presiding in high authority over the affairs of men. And if so, will not the man of piety and mercy receive tokens of favor, rather than the oppressive and cruel? Will not the Father of mercies ever approve that which resembles himself? Can any conclusion be more just? But we are not left to mere inference—we have certainty. "He that hath pity upon the poor, lendeth to the Lord; and that which he hath given will he pay him again." How beautiful is this promise! God makes himself debtor for every act of kindness to the poor! Who would not advance upon such credit? *God will pay him;* he whose goodness and whose resources are alike infinite, can never want the disposition or the means to repay every such gift. Again says God, "If there be among you a poor man of one of thy brethren, thou shalt not harden thine heart, nor shut thine hand from thy poor brother; but thou shalt open thine hand wide unto him, and shalt surely lend him sufficient for his need, in that which he wanteth. For this thing the Lord thy God shalt bless thee in all thy works, and in all that thou puttest thy hand unto." How easily can almighty Goodness accomplish this interesting promise! Permit me to add one more of equal, if not superior beauty: "Blessed is the man that considereth the poor: the Lord will deliver him in time of trouble. The Lord will preserve him, and keep him alive; and he shall be blessed upon the earth. The Lord will strengthen him upon the bed of languishing: thou wilt make all his bed in his sickness." Now, take an illustration. A terrible famine overspread the land of Israel. The prophet of God, faint and weary, craved at the hand of a widow a morsel of bread. "As the Lord liveth," said she, "I have naught but a handful of meal and a little oil in a cruse; and behold I am gathering two sticks, that I may go in and dress it for me and my son, that we may eat it and die. And the prophet said, Fear not; go and do as thou hast said; but make me a little cake first, and after make for thee and thy son. And she did so; and she and her house did eat many days. *And the barrel of meal wasted not, neither did the cruse of oil fail.*" "There is that scattereth and yet increaseth. The liberal shall be made fat, and he that watereth shall be watered again."

> "The quality of mercy is not strained;
> It droppeth as the dew from heaven
> Upon the place beneath. It is twice blessed;
> It blesseth him that gives and him that takes."

Though this promise may chiefly relate to the rewards which *God* will bestow, yet mercy often meets a corresponding reward from men. Whatever may be the circumstances or the mode of its exercise, it usually finds the same measure meted in return. Sympathy will be repaid by sympathy, kindness by kindness, and forgiveness by forgiveness. "Give," says our Savior, "and it shall be given unto you; good measure, pressed down, shaken together and running over, shall *men* give into your bosom."

3. *They are blessed with an interest in the affections and prayers of the objects of their compassion.*

Whatever the profane may think, this is not a blessing to be despised. It is often more to be valued than princely gifts, or the highest earthly good. There is not only a pleasure in doing good, but the blessings of the poor thrill the heart with a joy but little less than heaven. "The prayers of the righteous avail much." Sometimes, indeed, they secure to us what is far better than treasures of gold and silver. Let me show you how it is. In the western part of New York lived a pious, but deeply-afflicted man. Continued afflictions soon reduced him to abject poverty. Under these circumstances he was found by a kind-hearted, but irreligious gentleman. He was a man of wealth, and amply supplied the wants of this suffering family. "What," said the poor man to his wife one day, "what return can we make our kind benefactor? I know of nothing," he continued, "that we can do, but to pray that God may give him the true riches." For this he prayed without ceasing. Like Jacob, he had power with God. A few weeks afterward his friend, without any visible cause, publicly connected himself with the Church, and found the salvation of God. A revival of religion ensued, which resulted in the conversion of many precious souls. "Blessed are the merciful: for they shall obtain mercy."

4. *They shall obtain mercy in the day of the Lord Jesus.*

Solemn thought—"we must all appear before the judgment-seat of Christ!" There each must render his account to God. Before that dread tribunal "the deeds done in the body" will be investigated, and receive their just awards. How grand and awful will be the scenes of that day! The voice of the archangel and the trump of God—the descending Judge crowned with glory—the dead coming up from the long sleep of death—the heavens wrapped in flame—the elements melting with fervent heat—the earth and all that is therein, consumed by devouring fires: all these will invest that day with a pomp and majesty that will fill the stoutest heart with dismay. Who in that day will not feel the need of mercy? Then to meet the approving smile of God will itself be heaven. Amid these impressive scenes, transported with joy, and shining in the likeness of Christ, stand the *merciful*. Him they followed through the regeneration of life; they copied his example; they trod in his footsteps, and now they come to receive the rewards of infinite and everlasting mercy. Hear the Judge: "Come, ye blessed of my Father, inherit the kingdom prepared for you from the foundation of the world; for I was an hungered, and ye gave me meat: I was thirsty, and ye gave me drink: I was a stranger, and ye took me in: naked, and ye clothed me: I was sick, and ye visited me: in prison, and ye came unto me." Amazed at such commendation, they ask, "Lord, when saw we thee an hungered, and fed thee? or thirsty, and gave thee drink? when saw we thee a stranger, and took thee in? or naked, and clothed thee? or when saw we thee sick, or in prison, and came unto thee? And the King shall answer, and say unto them, Verily, I say unto you, Inasmuch as ye have done unto *one of the least of these my brethren*, ye have done it unto me. Enter ye into the joy of your Lord." In this manner, and before an assembled universe, will he acknowledge and reward their deeds of mercy—crowning them forever with the *mercy of our Lord Jesus Christ unto eternal life*. O, thou most merciful and compassionate Redeemer, make me like thyself—all meek—all gentle—all holy! O,

"Teach me to feel another's woe,
To hide the fault I see;
That mercy I to others show
That mercy show to me!"

LECTURE VII.

SIXTH BEATITUDE.

"Blessed are the pure in heart: for they shall see God." MATTHEW v, 8.

We have intimated, in a previous discourse, that the subject of our Savior's teaching was religion; not a new religion, but the old purified from the admixture of human error, divested of the cumbrous forms of a darker dispensation, and completed by additional revelations of doctrine and duty essential to salvation. Thus bestowed upon the world by him, it was pure and perfect. Entering the heart, it was to be an all-controlling and sanctifying principle, and its effects were to be visible in the tempers and deportment of all who bore his name. His religion is pre-eminently one of life and power; it has all the superiority that a vital and soul-purifying system can possibly possess over one of mere form and ceremony. Between two such systems there must be a wide and obvious distinction. "The one," says a pious author, "is the name, the other is the thing; the one is the body, the other is the soul; the former shows us the Christian upon canvas, the latter presents him alive and in motion." And yet, religion is not to be wholly divested of forms; for though they may be nothing by themselves, yet they render it more tangible, and even impressive, than it would be in their absence.

With men there has ever been a disposition to

rest in forms—to substitute them for life and spirituality. The Jews are an instance of this. When our Savior appeared, they had an imposing and splendid ritual; it was of Divine origin, and a speaking type of better things to come. But, dazzled with its pomp, they entirely overlooked its meaning, and contented themselves with the mere ceremony, the spiritual import of which was hidden from their eyes. They fasted much; they prayed long and often; they gave tithes of all; they avoided all external defilement, often washing their hands, and "holding, also, to the washing of pots, cups, brazen vessels, and tables"—forgetting, meanwhile, that the heart might be filled with every abomination and uncleanness. The consequence was, they appeared righteous unto men, but within were full of hypocrisy and iniquity. And are we not too much like them—wedded to outward forms, but strangers to the inward grace—ever varnishing the exterior, and loudly talking of purity, while, it may be, covetousness and pride, and kindred evils reign within? O, my brethren, let us lay to heart the pungent rebuke of Christ: "Woe unto you, scribes and Pharisees! for ye are like unto whited sepulchers, which, indeed, appear beautiful without, but within are full of dead men's bones and of all uncleanness." Deliverance from the plague of our hearts, is our first and highest duty.

"Blessed are the pure in heart." We are conducted at once, by this expression, to the nature and seat of true religion. Its nature is purity; "for the wisdom that cometh from above is first pure." "The wisdom of the world is earthly, sensual, and devilish;"

but true religion is heavenly, spiritual, and godlike. It purifies man; it exalts him to the fellowship of angels and the fruition of God. Its seat is the heart; it, therefore, subdues the will, calms the conscience, and sanctifies the affections; the kingdom of heaven is set up within. God reigns in the heart, and fills it with the purity and joy of his presence. Engrossing the chief points in the text, let us make three inquiries: What is purity of heart? is its attainment possible? and what are its rewards?

I. THEN, WHAT IS PURITY OF HEART?

A very brief negative view of the subject may, perhaps, contribute somewhat to more just conceptions of its nature and distinctive traits. First of all, then, it is not absolute purity—this belongs to the Divine nature alone; and it is as blasphemous as it is false, for man or angel to claim what is preeminently an attribute of the uncreated and infinite Jehovah. It does not exclude the possibility of temptation. Our Savior was holy, harmless, and undefiled—he was without any taint of sin; yet he was long and sorely tempted of Satan. And to whatever hights of holiness man may attain in the present life, he will suffer from the same crafty and malignant foe. Nor is it a state that precludes the possibility of falling. If Adam, in his primitive purity and perfection, could sin and fall, so may we, his degenerate and erring children. Both the possibility and dreadfulness of a lapse into sin, are announced by the apostle, in the following impressive language: "For if, after we have escaped the pollutions of the world through the knowledge of our Lord and Savior Jesus Christ, we are entangled therein and overcome, the latter end is worse than the beginning."

"The pure in heart," says that truly-eminent divine, Mr. Wesley, "are they whose hearts God hath purified even as he is pure; who are purified, through faith in the blood of Jesus, from every unholy affection; who, being cleansed from all filthiness of flesh and spirit, perfect holiness in the fear of God." These views are eminently evangelical and simple, and supply at once a beautiful definition and a life-like portrait of the pure in heart. Purity of heart, then, properly consists in a thorough inward change and complete renovation of the heart. The Psalmist prays, "Create in me a clean heart, O God, and renew a right spirit within me." It is, therefore, the product of a new creation—a creation so real and entire, that old things pass away, and *all* things become new.

1. *It implies, in the first place, salvation from sin—its guilt, its power, and especially its pollution.*

None enjoy the latter who have not been made partakers of the former. All such, therefore, have been "freely justified by grace through the redemption that is in Jesus;" they have been delivered from the galling yoke and service of sin; "sin hath no more dominion over them, for they are not under the law, but under grace." But purity of heart essentially implies deliverance from its *pollution.* Sin not only burdens the heart with guilt—it *defiles;* it renders the heart impure, and utterly unfits it for the enjoyment of God and the society of the heavenly world. The Scriptures, therefore, represent it by every form and figure of speech expressive of impurity. They speak of it as wounds, bruises, and putrefying sores; as leprosy and plague; as the rottenness and corruption of the grave. It defiles every thing it touches; because of it, the whole creation groaneth, and the beautiful world around us is doomed, like the house of the leper, to perish, because of the defilement of its possessor. Some, I know, plead for the goodness of their hearts, and contend that human corruption is not from within, but from without—the effect of vicious training and example. Need I say, that this is in direct contradiction to the language of the Son of God? "From *within*," says he, "out of the *heart* of men, proceedeth evil thoughts, adulteries, murders, thefts, covetousness, wickedness, deceit, lasciviousness, an evil eye, blasphemy, pride, foolishness; all these evil things come from *within* and *defile* the man." Now, as sin alone constitutes moral defilement, its removal is essential to the purity of the heart; its deep stains *must* be washed out, or we remain forever impure, and forever lost. How interesting, then, to him who feels the plague of his heart, is that heaven-devised system, which not only proposes but provides for a full and complete deliverance from the reign and inbeing of sin!

2. *It implies the presence and growing perfection of the fruits of the Spirit.*

True religion does not end in negatives; it has a positive character and positive graces. No man clears his garden of weeds, but that he may set it with useful plants, or adorn it with pleasant flowers. God requires us to dispossess our corruptions; but it is that the heart may receive new inhabitants. It is not enough that it be emptied and swept—it must be garnished with celestial furniture. We are, indeed, to be saved from our inbred and manifold evils; but it is that heavenly virtues may rise up and shine in their places. By a beautiful figure of speech, the apostle calls them fruits of the Spirit; "they are love, joy, peace, long-suffering, gentleness, goodness, faith, meekness, patience, temperance." The heart having been purified from sin by a Divine washing, it becomes "an habitation of God through the Spirit;" even as God hath said, "I will dwell in them and walk in them." As a Spirit of light, purity, and fruitfulness, he occupies and pervades the soul, and these heavenly virtues become the proper fruits and manifestations of his indwelling presence. Love, eldest born, leads the train, and sheds over every faculty of the soul its sweet and sanctifying power; the others follow by necessary sequence, to bless the heart, and beautify the life with every thing that is lovely and of good report. These fruits first appear in our regeneration; and at this period the work of our purification also begins. Then we are born of the Spirit, and become partakers of the Divine nature; and these Divine affections begin to unfold themselves as the gracious effects and certain proofs of a renewed nature. Thenceforth they exist in growing perfection; advancing to higher degrees of maturity, till the soul is filled with the "fruits of righteousness," and is prepared "to stand in the presence of God, not having spot or wrinkle, or any such thing." "Whatsoever things are true; whatsoever things are pure;

whatsoever things are excellent; if there be any virtue, and if there be any praise," they must ever be regarded as characteristic of the pure in heart, and as entering essentially into the nature of this condition.

3. *Purity of heart implies corresponding sanctity of life.*

He that saith he abideth in him, ought himself, also, so to walk, even as he walked; that is, he who professes to be united to Christ, and to be pure of heart, ought to live and act as he did; his life should be a transcript of the Savior's, a constant outbeaming of the purity that reigns within. A holy life essentially includes the following things. First. An avoidance of every thing that would tend to sully or defile the heart. In such a world as ours, so deeply fallen, so rife with sin, a very sea of corruption, there is constant danger of pollution. A thousand sources exist around and in us: among the most common are impure thoughts and desires, evil associates, unlawful business, and forbidden pleasures; and he who would keep his spirit pure, must watch and pray, and resist, in the strength of grace, their fatal influence. I do not say that we must abandon human society, and bury ourselves in caves and cloisters, the more certainly to attain eminent degrees of purity. Monkish seclusion is not a means of holiness; on the contrary, we are called to the activities of life; we should mingle with its scenes. Yet must we diligently watch and pray that we enter not into temptation. Thus may we be *in* the world, and yet not *of* the world, moving in our several providential spheres, and yet keep our garments pure from defilement. A holy life includes the government of the tongue. Perhaps in no way does the condition of the heart develop itself more than through the medium of the tongue: "Out of the abundance of the heart the mouth speaketh." Not more certainly does the magnetic needle indicate the position of the pole, than does the tongue the moral state of the heart; and upon no subject does the Bible speak with more energy and distinctness: "If any man among you seem to be religious, and bridleth not his tongue, this man's religion is vain." Religion is designed to bring the entire man under its purifying sway; no matter how elevated may be our profession, a single unsubdued and reigning sin will demonstrate its falsity. If any sin is indulged, if the tongue is unsubdued, it will show that the *seat* of the evil has not been reached, and that the soul has not been brought under the reign of purity and love. "The tongue," says an inspired apostle, "is a fire, a world of iniquity; it defileth the whole body." Such is the position and relation which it occupies, that it stains and pollutes the whole moral system. On the contrary, "if a man offend not in word, the same is a perfect man." His chaste conversation indicates a pure heart. The world, even, will repose confidence in the profession of such a man; while no one can be deceived by the pretensions of the blasphemer, the man of obscene lips, or the vain and irreverent trifler. In fine, a holy life includes conformity to the Divine will as a rule of conduct. Obedience is the essential fruit of a renewed nature. A pure heart alone can fully appreciate and delight in the law of God; its proper language is, "O, how I love thy law; yea, thy law is within my heart; I love thy commandments above gold; thy testimonies have I taken as an heritage forever: for they are the rejoicing of my heart." This obedience is universal. It has respect to all the will of God. What that will prohibits is abandoned; what it enjoins is performed with pleasure—"I can do all things through Christ which strengtheneth me." It is affectionate—love reigns within; and, therefore, it is not the service of a slave or a hireling, but of a loving, happy child.

> "'Tis love that makes our cheerful feet
> In swift obedience move."

It is persevering. It continues in storm as well as in sunshine, and is equally constant when driven of fierce winds and adverse tides, as when sailing upon a tranquil sea. Such are some of the peculiar features of the life when under the promptings and control of a pure heart. We are now prepared to enter upon our second inquiry.

II. IS THIS STATE OF GRACE ATTAINABLE—MAY WE POSSESS PURE AND HOLY HEARTS?

No inquiry can be more important than this, and I know of none that admits of a more satisfactory solution. To this question, then, I answer distinctly and without hesitation, Yes, it is attainable; it is our privilege to be pure in heart. The evidence of this I derive from several sources.

1. *It is a condition of eternal life.*

Christians of every name concur in this, and such is the uniform doctrine of the Bible. "Who," says the Psalmist, "shall ascend into the hill of the Lord, and who shall stand in his holy place?" The response is, "He that hath clean hands and a pure heart." This language may be allusive, but the great moral truth inculcated is obvious, and is re-uttered in the most direct manner by the apostle, when he says, "Without holiness no man shall see the Lord." Now, can we for one moment think, much less believe, that the rewards of heaven are suspended upon terms impracticable and impossible? Do such thoughts harmonize with the character and perfections of God? Are they worthy of Him who devoted his well-beloved Son to the death of the cross; and who has assured us that it is his good pleasure to save us all? Do they accord with the provisions and free invitations of the Gospel of his Son? No. Of nothing am I more certain than that, if he requires purity of heart as the condition of final blessedness, it is attainable. The simple fact that it is a demand of infinite justice, truth, and goodness, demonstrates this.

2. *To secure this great blessing to us was one object of the atonement.*

Indeed, every thing connected with the sublime mission and work of Christ looks to this, and is intended to promote this. His name. "Thou shalt call his name Jesus," said the holy angel, "for he shall save his people from their sins;" not only their guilt and penalty, but their defilement. In assuming this name, he intimates that he wishes us to regard him chiefly in this character. He comes into the world bearing a name, which proclaims him the world's Savior; and now that he is gone to his throne, he seems to say, "My name is Jesus yet, I am a Savior still. Come, ye sinful and vile, ye polluted and unholy, I am 'able to save you even unto the uttermost.'" His entrance into our world. "I am come," said he, "that ye might have life." An essential element of the life he offers is purity. "For this purpose," says St. John, "was the Son of God manifested, that he might destroy the works of the devil." Sin, in all its various forms, is appropriately his work; he was the first sinner; and the human heart, in its guilt, and enslavement, and pollution, exhibits the frightful ravages of his power. But, thank God! there is one higher and mightier than the prince of evil: Immanuel is his name; he entered the world as a conqueror; he comes to liberate the captive soul; nor shall he fail or be discouraged till he shall have achieved the mighty conquest, and irreparably overturned the kingdom of sin and Satan. But especially his death. The relation which this bears to our purity, is that of cause and effect; and to provide for our purification was the design of the sacrifice he offered upon the cross. He came to put away sin by the sacrifice of himself. "For the bodies of those beasts, whose blood is brought into the sanctuary by the high-priest for sin, are burned without the camp. Wherefore Jesus, that he might *sanctify the people with his own blood*, suffered without the gate." The apostles love to linger upon this theme. In tracing out the design of the atonement, their very words seem to glow with hope and joy. "Christ also loved the Church," says St. Paul, "and gave himself for it, that he might *sanctify and cleanse* it with the washing of water by the word; and that he might present it to himself a glorious Church, not having spot, or wrinkle, or any such thing, but that it should be holy, and without blemish." And again, he says, "He gave himself for us, that he might redeem us from all iniquity, and purify unto himself a peculiar people, zealous of good works." The legal sacrifices, even, availed for external defilement. How much more shall the blood of Christ, who, through the eternal Spirit, offered himself to God, purge your conscience from dead works, to serve the living God! Such evidence should silence every cavil, and banish every doubt. The very heart should thrill with joy when we think how fully all our depravity is provided for in the atonement of the Son of God. O, when I see him stooping from infinite hights to the form and condition of a servant; when I hear him called by the name of Jesus; when I see him bleeding upon the cross, and opening a fountain for uncleanness, and sending forth his Spirit, and instituting ordinances, and all for one specific purpose, I will not, I *can not* doubt that it is my privilege to be pure and holy!

3. *Look now at the promises in relation to this subject.*

"The promises," says an old divine, "are a precious book, written by the finger of God, and every leaf drops myrrh and honey. They are golden vessels, in which are treasured the brightest jewels God has to bestow;" and one of the richest and the brightest of these jewels is purity of heart. This he has engaged, by covenant and promise, to bestow on all his believing children. Opening the Old Testament, and entering a dispensation comparatively imperfect, we find the following gracious overtures:

"I will turn my hand upon thee, and will *purely purge away thy dross.* Though your sins be as scarlet,* they shall be as *white as snow;* though they be red like crimson, *they shall be as wool.*" And again: "I will sprinkle clean water upon you, and *ye shall be clean;* from all your idols and from all your filthiness will I cleanse you." True it is, that this language is highly figurative, but the most ordinary mind can scarcely misapprehend it. In the New Testament we shall find still more clearly-written promises. In the view of St. Paul, the Divine arrangement unfolded in the Gospel is a better covenant than the old, and established upon better promises. These better promises relate directly to our deliverance from the power and defilement of sin, and form the reason and the basis of his ardent prayers and urgent exhortations in regard to its attainment. The following passages will represent, in some degree, the nature and extent of the stipulations of this better covenant: "If we walk in the light, as he is in the light, we have fellowship one with another, and the blood of Jesus Christ his Son cleanseth us from *all* sin. If we confess our sins, he is faithful and just to forgive us our sins, and to cleanse us from *all* unrighteousness." "Having, therefore," says St. Paul, "these promises, dearly beloved, let us cleanse ourselves from all filthiness, both of the flesh and spirit, perfecting holiness in the fear of God."

4. *But let us take facts, and this will give additional strength to the argument.*

Many have enjoyed it; many do now. Indeed, all do, up to the measure of their faith in the blood of Christ. In regard to the simple fact, there were such in the days of the apostles. Hence says St. Paul, in addressing some, "But now being made free from sin, and become servants to God, ye have your fruit unto holiness, and the end everlasting life." Of others he says, "Ye are washed, ye are sanctified, ye are justified in the name of the Lord Jesus, and by the Spirit of our God." And again, speaking of the equality of privilege between Jew and Gentile, an apostle says, "God hath put no difference between us and them, purifying their hearts by faith." There are such now; but where shall we find them—in what Church? By what name are they distinguished? I answer, wherever God's true people are found. They are not known by party names or denominational peculiarities, not even by a faultless creed or a sounding profession, but by the purity of their conversation, and the spotless sanctity of their lives. "The tree is known by its fruit." Wherever there is a humble, holy, devoted life, there you find a pure heart, and only there. As a pure fountain sends forth refreshing and healthful streams, so does the renovated heart uniformly exhibit holy tempers, and a holy life. Such is the decision both of enlightened reason and the word of God. I repeat, there are such *now;* they walk with God, having the testimony that they please him; they have put on the Lord Jesus, being crucified with him, that the body of sin might be destroyed. These, my brethren, are the living, breathing epistles of Christ, written not with ink, but with the Spirit of the living God; not in tables of stone, but in fleshy tables of the heart.

Here I will pause for a moment to drop an inquiry or two.

Do any of you pant for the clean heart and the pure spirit? One of the first things necessary is a sense of your inbred sin; the deep corruption of your heart. But I trust you already feel this, and therefore sigh for deliverance. You have long prayed, "Create in me a clean heart, O God, and renew a right spirit within me." Your next, your *immediate* duty is confidence in the blood of atonement, and simple reliance upon it. That blood can make the foulest clean. So thorough is your pollution; so deep and desperate the defilement of sin, that no ceremonial appliances will do. No,

> "None but *Jesus*, *none* but Jesus
> Can do helpless sinners good."

In him tnere *is* a remedy, an all-cleansing fountain opened in his most precious blood. Here the guiltiest and the vilest have found salvation, and here each and all of you may wash your sins away. Go, then, to him. He is a mighty Savior; able and willing to save unto the uttermost. Turn to an instance in the eighth chapter. When he had descended from the mount, there met him a wretched and outcast leper. Bowing at the feet of the Savior he said, "Lord, if thou wilt, thou canst make me clean." At once the Savior stretched forth his hand, saying, "I will." What a thrill of joy run through the heart of that man! And does he not say the same to you? He does. But look at the result. "Be thou clean," says Jesus, and immediately his leprosy was cleansed. What a proof, both of his ability and willingness to save! Go, then, to him.

Cast thyself upon him in humble but fearless trust. Claim his promises; claim a *present* salvation. He will not, he *can not*, turn you away unrelieved.

> "Thou dying Lamb! thy precious blood
> Shall never lose its power,
> Till all the ransomed Church of God
> Are saved, to sin no more."

III. Let us now contemplate the reward of the pure in heart.

I need scarcely say, in the language of the text, that such are blessed. Were I to pause here, you could not go away with any other impression. Such must be happy. Their hearts purified from sin, which always darkens and afflicts the soul, they *must* be happy. And no reverses of fortune, no assaults of earth or hell, can essentially mar their peace. It is, however, in the grandeur of their privilege that we especially see their reward—"Blessed are the pure in heart: for *they shall see God.*" No human mind, however gifted or far-reaching in its powers of thought, can explore the hidden wealth of this promise. We can only realize its meaning when we stand in the presence of God and enjoy the glories of the beatific vision. We may, nevertheless, without presumption, make a few plain and practical observations.

"They shall see God." There is a sense in which all shall see him. "Behold, he cometh with clouds, and every eye shall see him, and they also which pierced him: and all kindreds of the earth shall wail because of him." See him, not as a Friend and Savior, but as a righteous Judge, coming to punish the ungodly, and raise his people to immortal honors! O what multitudes, when they behold that lovely face beaming through the parted clouds, will call for rocks and mountains to fall on them, and hide them from the face of Him that sitteth upon the throne!

But our Savior here speaks of it as a token of favor, and as constituting an exalted reward. And St. John, in one of his beautiful descriptions of heavenly happiness, says they shall see his face, and his name shall be in their foreheads. To see the face of one, or to stand in his presence, were, among the Jews, terms expressive of great favor. So here, to see the face of God, means to be his friends and favorites, and to dwell with him forever in the final abodes of purity and joy.

Furthermore, the phrase, to see God, in the language of the critics, is a Hebraism for the enjoyment of God. Thus our Savior says, "Except a man be born again he can not *see* the kingdom of God;" that is, he can neither inherit nor enjoy the present privileges or future bliss of the saints in light. This had an impressive type in the Jewish ceremonial. A person who was legally pure, was permitted to enter the sanctuary and worship as in the presence of God; while the defiled and impure were excluded from the sacred precincts, as unfit to appear in the presence of unspotted purity and holiness.

1. *There is an interesting sense in which this reward is enjoyed at present.*

The pure in heart see and enjoy God in the works of his hands. The visible universe is full of God. All its vast variety is the production of his skill, the token of his benevolence, and the imperfect image of his greatness. But amid these wondrous scenes God is unknown and unfelt by the gross and sensual mind. True, it may perceive the forms of beauty and the traces of infinite wisdom, but it neither feels nor rejoices in his presence. Surrounded, indeed, with suns and systems, in all their pomp and glory, the *fool* hath said in his heart there is *no* God. It is otherwise with the man of purified heart and mind. He walks no where but he meets and communes with God. To him "the heavens declare the glory of God, and the firmament showeth his handiwork." When his eye measures yonder heavens, or glides over the hills and valleys of this beautiful world, his heart pulsates with rapture. When the dew sparkles upon the grass, a kindred tear drops from his eye. It is not the tear of sorrow, but of inward delight and joy, which no language can express. He meets the Father of spirits, going forth to renew the face of the earth and fill all hearts with food and gladness. He meets and adores.

"These are thy glorious works, Parent of good,
Almighty! Thine this universal frame,
Thus wondrous fair; thyself how wondrous then!"

He enjoys God in the operations and comforts of his grace. "He that loveth me," says Jesus, "shall be loved of my Father, and I will love him, and will manifest myself to him." That grace brought him from darkness to light, translating him from the kingdom of Satan unto the kingdom of God's dear Son. When dead in trespasses and sins it quickened him, and raised him up to sit with Christ in heavenly places. The love of God is shed abroad in his heart, itself a source of ineffable delight. He is exalted to heavenly fellowships, having come to an innumerable company of angels, to the spirits of just men made perfect, to God the judge of all, and to Jesus the mediator of the new covenant. He enjoys the witness of the Spirit. It abides within his heart a *comforter*, the seal of his sonship, and the earnest of joys to come. He enjoys the Divine presence—"I will never leave thee nor forsake thee." This compensates for the loss of every earthly good, the absence of every earthly friend. It disperses every gloom, cheers in every sorrow, sustains in every trial, and even sheds, upon the dark valley of death, the holy light of triumphant joy. From these sources arise a purity and a plenitude of bliss, that nothing in the universe can excel but heaven.

2. *But this promise looks to the future world for its highest fulfillment.*

It is there in God's immediate presence, and where the light of his countenance shines in all its effulgence, that this promise is to be realized in its full meaning. All that is seen or known of him in the present state, dwindles into nothing compared with the grand disclosures of the heavenly world. "To see God as he reveals himself to the spirits of the just made perfect in heaven, has ever been the crowning hope of good men, and formed their loftiest conceptions of future felicity." Amid the most distressing calamities, the suffering patriarch looked up and said, "Yet in my flesh shall I *see* God." In language glowing with immortal hope, the apostle exclaims, "It doth not yet appear what we shall be; but we know that when he shall appear we shall be like him, for we shall *see him as he is*." One of the elders of heaven, surveying the shining ranks of the glorified, says, "These are they which came out of great tribulation, and have washed their robes and made them white in the blood of the Lamb. Therefore are they *before the throne of God*, and serve him day and night in his temple. They stand in his immediate presence, where they see the King in his beauty, and behold his face in righteousness."

The beatific vision will open to the soul a source of pure and transporting bliss. Even in this cold and distant world there are seasons of heavenly sunshine and ecstatic rapture. Sometimes, indeed, the soul takes the wings of faith and love, and, soaring away, seems to mingle in the company and songs of the better land. But these are only the streams; and

"If such the sweetness of the *streams*,
What must the *fountain* be?"

Infinitely superior. The joys of the soul, when its communings with God are deepest and sweetest, are to the joys above but the twilight of heaven, the early dawn of a perfect day. Look at its descriptions: it is entering into the joy of our Lord; it is being presented before the presence of his glory with exceeding joy—"his presence, where there is fullness of joy and pleasures for evermore." These enjoyments will be *perpetual*. "Permanency adds bliss to bliss." Every thing is mutable here. There, every thing is permanent. Is it life? It is eternal. Is it salvation? It is everlasting. Is it a crown? It fadeth not away. They are *increasing* as well as permanent. Progress is the great law of Christianity. Every thing pertaining to the Christian is progressive. His character, his knowledge, his happiness—all are in a state of advancement, and even more in the future than in the present world. Freed from this mortal clog, the mind will then operate with a freedom and facility at present unknown—"Now we see through a glass darkly, but then face to face." The perfections of God, the wonders of the universe, the sufferings of Christ, and the riches of redeeming mercy will open boundless fields of contemplation, where the soul shall expatiate with constant and endless accessions of strength, illumination, and joy. O glorious prospect! When shall the soul, freed from its prison-house of clay, soar to its native heaven? The day of your redemption draweth nigh. See the ransomed spirit; it mingles and sings with angels. It has received the crown of glory, the palm of conquest, and the robe of white, washed in the blood of the Lamb. No more pain, no more toil, no more sorrow;

> "For sin, the source of mortal woe,
> Can never enter there."

I shall close with a brief address to three characters.

1. The formalist. You have the name, but not the life and power of religion. Can you imagine that your condition is a safe one? Have you not every reason to believe that it is one of alarming danger? God requires a spiritual religion—a pure heart. He demands of you a life consecrated to his service; a life of cheerful and unremitting obedidience to his will. Have you a heart thus renewed and filled with the fruits of righteousness? You

have not. You regard such an experience as fanatical. But what is the testimony of St. Paul? "He is not a Jew who is one outwardly; neither is that circumcision which is outward in the flesh: but he is a Jew which is one inwardly; and circumcision is that of the heart, in the spirit and not in the letter; whose praise is not of men but of God." And what is the testimony of our Lord? "Except a man be born again he can not see the kingdom of God." To rest in mere forms, is like a man laying down to repose on the foam of the ocean, only to sink and perish. Rest in the blood of Christ. Seek purity of heart, without which you will forever be excluded from the company and the happiness of heaven.

2. There is another class who feel the need and are seeking the blessing of purity. Let no sense of sin or helplessness dishearten you. Jesus died to redeem you. He shed his blood to wash away your sins. He waits to impart to you all its healing virtues. This should banish fear, and inspire living hope and confidence, "He that believeth shall be saved." Falling on your bended knees make this your prayer, Lord help me, Lord deliver me—wash me thoroughly from my iniquity, and cleanse me from my sin. Simply trust the virtue of his blood, and soon thou shalt hear more than an angel's voice, saying, "Thine iniquity is taken away, and thy sin is purged."

3. Those who have realized this heavenly washing. Remember that you are not above the reach of temptation or the danger of falling into sin. You still need, and need every moment, the merit of his death. Has that precious blood saved you?

Its continued application alone can keep you clean. Walk in harmony with your profession. Be humble. Boast not of your attainments. Rejoice evermore, but rejoice with trembling. Be not high-minded, but fear. Let your life speak. God and man demand of you a consistent and holy life rather than a sounding profession. Go forward; there are rich fields of experience yet to explore, and delectable mountains yet to ascend. Go forward; the prize of your high calling yet glitters in the distance. Go forward, nor pause in your upward career till you stand among the redeemed, an everlasting monument of the purifying blood of Christ.

LECTURE VIII.

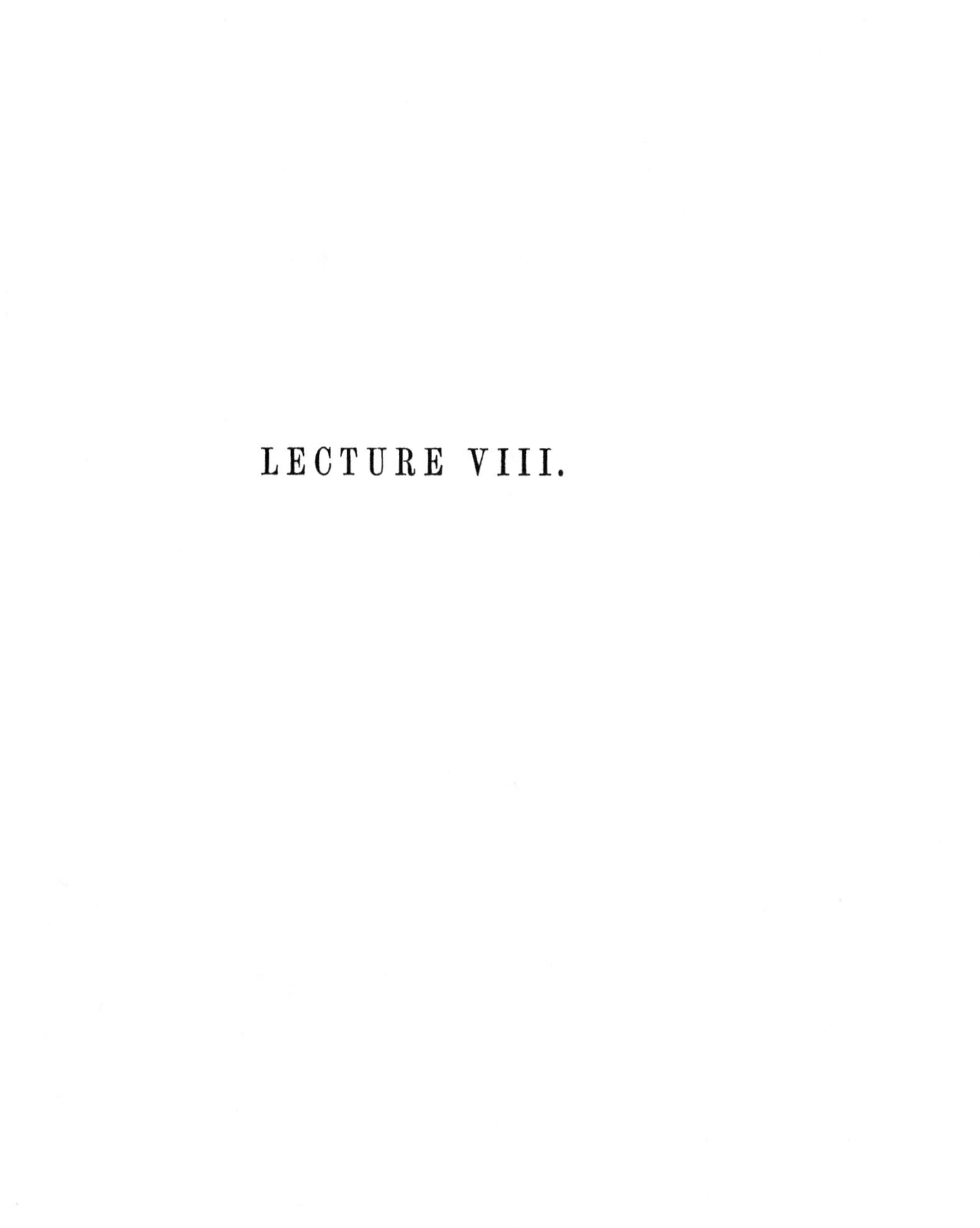

SEVENTH BEATITUDE.

"Blessed are the peace-makers: for they shall be called the children of God." MATTHEW v, 9.

THE existence of strife in the world is a direct and palpable proof of the corruption of human nature. This is its proper source; it can flow from no other. It could not proceed from a holy nature, no more than poisonous streams could issue from a healthful fountain. It is a consequence of the fall, and accordingly displayed itself early in the history of the race. Among the first statements in regard to the condition of man, we read, "that the earth was filled with violence." Succeeding history shows but little abatement. In proportion as the human family have multiplied and spread, variance and strife have increased, till of the race it may be said, "they are hateful and hating one another." Nor have the evils been slight or transient that have poured from this dreadful source. On the contrary, they have rolled over the world like streams of burning lava, destroying, in their course, the harmony and the happiness of the world. The progress of mankind has been marked, in every age, by envy, debate, deceit; by malignity, spitefulness, and bloodshed. The tender ties of kindred have been rudely severed. The bands of society have been rent by contending factions. The flames of war have been kindled, and fire and sword have desolated the earth. Such are the leading facts of human history.

Now, a religion suited to man must provide an adequate remedy for these evils. It may, therefore, be concluded that a religion from God would not propose less than a complete revolution of the human heart—a revolution so thorough as to be equivalent to a new creation; so far subduing the carnal mind and renewing the spirit of man, that at length every heart should vibrate in unison, and peace and harmony return to bless the world. Such a religion was that taught by the Son of God. When the "herald angels" proclaimed his birth, they sung in joyful strains, "Glory to God in the highest, on earth peace and good will to men." And how proper the anthem! "For the kingdom of God is not meat and drink, but righteousness, *peace*, and joy in the Holy Ghost." Accordingly, when it enters the heart it melts it into tenderness; it subdues the will; it "purges out the old leaven of malice and wickedness;" it harmonizes the passions; it purifies and warms the affections, and fills the soul with peace and good will to men. Having thus renewed, it sends him forth a peaceful spirit into a warring world. His proper work now is to heal discussions, reconcile contending factions, pour oil upon the troubled sea of human passion, and banish enmity and discord from the earth. Both his warrant and his comfort in the prosecution of this work is to be found in the language of the Savior, "Blessed are the peace-makers: for they shall be called the children of God." Selecting one individual as the representative of the entire class, let us,

I. Investigate his principles.

Principles may be regarded as the sources of action, and as giving tone and complexion to character. Whether, therefore, we would estimate the character of another, or form our own to goodness and virtue, we must never lose sight of those great elements which develop themselves in the character and conduct of men. In a character so excellent and beneficial as that to which our attention is here directed, we may expect to find principles equally remarkable for their peculiarity and excellence; not such as are common to the multitude, but to the few; indeed, to those alone whose hearts have been brought under the influence of grace, and whose lives harmonize with the will of God. Two great principles will be found to actuate the peace-maker; and every movement in his high career of benevolence may be referred to these as their proper spring and fountain.

1. *The first is love to God.*

This is not a native principle of the heart; it is not brought into the world with us; it is purely of divine origin—it is from God. It implies a state of reconciliation and friendship with him, and lives and glows only in a renewed heart. The Bible speaks upon no subject more frequently, or with more energy, than the natural enmity and alienation of the heart. Though love, in our primitive state, was the great reigning principle, its dethronement, at present, is complete. This fact alone accounts for the strong language of inspiration in regard to our present condition, "The carnal mind is enmity against God; for it is not subject to the law of God, neither indeed can be." We are, therefore, alienated, and enemies in our mind, by wicked works. No act, no *thought* of man flows from love to God, for it has no existence in his heart; enmity reigns there, and of such depth and power as to place man in direct conflict with his Maker. Now, in the renewal of the heart by the Holy Spirit, this enmity is slain, and we are reconciled to God; we have peace with God through our Lord Jesus Christ; and now the love of God first springs up within the heart. "We love him because he first loved us." This principle now becomes a new source of feeling and action, powerfully influential upon the heart and life. It sweetens the temper, it calms the unquiet passions, it chastens the affections, and so controls the life as to make it a speaking illustration of the "beauty of holiness."

This principle binds the soul to God; it makes it one with him. Under its influence it adopts his will as its rule of action, and his glory as its high pursuit. It sympathizes with his purposes in the extermination of sin, and the diffusion of holiness and happiness through the universe. It warms the soul with generous impulses, it expands and elevates its views, it inspires it with ardent desires to advance the Divine glory, and secures to the purpose and the effort, though unsuccessful, the approbation of God and the assurance of reward. Without it the soul has no stimulus, and no power. Like a bird shorn of its wings, all its efforts to rise above mere selfish aims are fruitless. The "Christian's Pattern," far above its reach, is unattained and unattainable. We only begin the imitation of Christ in his excellences of character, and in his benevolent career, when we secure this principle of love to God in our souls.

2. *The second principle, distinguishing the peace-maker, is love to man.*

Love to God, we are divinely taught, is the first and the great command. The second in importance and usefulness is love to our neighhor. "On these two," says the Savior, "hang all the law and the prophets." They comprehend what Moses, in the law, and the prophets have spoken; and to produce the highest degree of happiness, to bind men together in sweet and lasting brotherhood, and then unite all to God, nothing more is necessary than to bring them under the control of these two great principles. Love to man comprehends, among other things, an ardent desire to do him good as we have opportunity, in "body, mind, and estate;" not because he is my relative or friend, not because he is of my creed or nation, but because he is man, made in the image of God, and redeemed by the blood of his Son. In its action it oversteps party bounds and denominational distinctions; it claims a sympathy in the well-being of every man; it embraces all in its "wide arms of love," and speaks a language understood and felt by men in every clime: "*Peace on earth and good will to men.*" No one can fail to perceive the relation which this principle bears to the conduct of the peace-maker, and that the character itself can have no existence in the absence of this element. To this is to be traced as its proper source every benevolent effort, every peace measure, every enterprise that would terminate the existence of strife, and restore the reign of peace and innocence to the world.

"Love," says the apostle, "worketh no ill to his neighbor." On the contrary, it seeks to do him good; it prompts to justice, truth, and benevolence, and holds in check those baser passions which engender strife, and flood the land with bitterness. Were the law of love engraved on every heart; did it control the conduct of men, what a change would come over society! Falsehood and detraction would cease; sly insinuation and ribald insult would be unknown; and the gossip and the tattler, those firebrands of mischief, would hide themselves for very shame. The bands of a holy brotherhood would bind the nations; men would dwell together in unity, and the social atmosphere would glow with the brightness and blessedness of heaven. Such, then, are the two great principles which distinguish the peace-maker—love to God and love to man. They form the basis of his character; they give impulse and direction to his efforts, and, in their reflex influence, pour upon his heart pure and abiding joys. Let us now,

II. Observe his practice.

"Blessed are the peace-*makers*." And here we are to contemplate him in action, and see the living embodiment of those principles which, when carried out in our intercourse with men, constitute that rare but God-like character denominated the peace-maker.

1. *And first, let us regard him in his several fields of benevolent effort.*

See him in the family. Families exist by Divine

appointment, and are especially designed to be the centers of purity and love. From these delightful sources refining influences are to flow out, spreading beyond the home circle to beautify and gladden the face of society. Nothing on earth furnishes a fitter type of heaven, than a family where peace presides and love attunes every heart in unison; angels look with delight upon it, and God himself delights to dwell there.

And yet, how often are families the scenes of rudeness and ill-humor, of wrangling and strife! Those who dwell under the same roof, sit at the same table, and are connected by the most tender relationships, are often seen exchanging angry looks and bitter words. The various and conflicting tempers of children often render it difficult to maintain domestic peace; one is petulant, another proud, a third envious, a fourth sullen. These are the true elements of discord, and not unfrequently embroil the family, and hang around it like a dark and wrathful cloud. Amid such a scene, the peacemaker is an angel of mercy. His influence there is salutary as the dew of Hermon, and refreshing as the odor of a rich perfume; and no one can so fully exhibit this character of the Christian parent. In the very nature of things he must be better acquainted with the members of the family than others. He knows their qualities of mind and heart; he has studied their moral constitution, and can adapt himself to their peculiarities; he is to them in God's stead; his voice is the voice of love, but not less of authority, which, while it inspires reverence, wins by its gentleness and love.

Under his control the family moves in unity and concord; the quarrels that distract other households are arrested by his kindly interference, and the passions that prompt them held in check by the blended influence of authority and love. The government of such a parent is not maintained by harshness or reserve, by the terror of the rod or the severity of punishment, but by the mightier influence of a wholesome discipline and an example of correct Christian deportment.

See him in the Church. Here, if any where upon earth, we should expect to find peace. As the Church professes a religion of peace, and stands before the world the visible representative of the meek Son of God, we should expect this spirit to pervade and control all her movements. But, alas! it has not been always so. Debates and divisions have sometimes destroyed the harmony of the "body of Christ," and rent in sunder the bonds of brotherly-love. The school of Christ has been the school of disputation and cavil. Prating impertinence and unblushing forwardness have here struggled for pre-eminence, and rival factions, led on by spiritual demagogues, have turned it into an arena of conflict and strife. So different are the tastes and habits of men; so great the variety of intellect and feeling; so various the modes of education and the character of temperament, that there is constant danger of collision and discord. The unsanctified affections and tempers of men are always fruitful of evil, and, existing as they often do in the professed followers of Christ, frequently display themselves in disagreement and contention, a result as hostile to the spirit, as it is disgraceful to the name of religion. Here, then, is a legitimate field for the labors of the peace-maker; and it is pleasing to contemplate him in his God-like career. Having imbibed the spirit and temper of the Gospel, he stands aloof from the scene of wrangling and variance; he has put off anger, wrath, and malice, and has "put on charity, which is the bond of perfectness;" he can not, therefore, participate in the work of discord; he counsels peace, and with unremitting zeal seeks to allay the demon-spirit of strife, and reunite the broken links of Christian fellowship and love. Such a man in the Church, be he rich or poor, wise or ignorant, is above all price. In him we see displayed the excellency of the Gospel; he stands before the world the bright embodiment of its beautiful spirit and principles. O, when shall this lovely character be displayed in every disciple of Jesus? When shall the spirit of discord be banished from the Church, and her sons and daughters dwell together in unity?

"O let us take a softer mold,
Blended and gathered into Thee;
Under one Shepherd make one fold,
Where all is love and harmony."

See him in community. And here he moves with the same gentleness and grace which distinguish him in the family and in the Church; and here, too, opens before him a wide field of pious and benevolent effort. It is not a rare occurrence, that neighborhoods and communities become scenes of contention and strife, disgraceful to humanity, and ending in riot and bloodshed. Some persons are censorious; they are perpetually finding fault; they see every thing through the green glasses of prejudice, and hence every object is discolored, if not distorted. Every thing is wrong; every body is at fault; themselves form the only exception—they of course are right. Such men utter no language but that of complaint and crimination; they fret and scold; they are a kind of social iceberg; the very atmosphere grows cold around them, and spreads a chill throughout the circle of their influence. Reciprocal irritation and blame succeed, till at length the family or the entire community is embroiled. Some again are contentious, and can only live amid the excitement of debate; they flourish best in a heated atmosphere, which, in morals as in nature, usually breeds contagion and death. This is an evil spirit, overbearing and tyrannical; it will have its own way, or else it will sacrifice friendship and the best interests of mankind. How often is the harmony of society, the unity of benevolent enterprise, plans of internal improvement, and commercial prosperity broken up by this hateful propensity! "For as coals are to burning coals, and wood to fire, so is a contentious man to kindle strife." And the beginning of strife in communities is like the letting out of waters; little by little is the crevice enlarged and the channel widened, till the rushing waters sweep away the embankments, and flood the land with destruction. Others are slanderous—the meanest part of this class are too cowardly to make an open attack; they never make charges; they deal in doubts and surmises. The very tones of their voice, and the expression of their countenance, excites distrust and awakens suspicion. You could meet an open, manly attack; but how can you deny a mysterious look, or refute a sinister glance? These are the very worst of traducers. I had rather meet a bear robbed of her whelps, than such a skulking hound.

> "Who stabs my name, would stab my person too,
> Did not the hangman's rope lie in the way."

Some are malicious and lustful. "From whence," says the apostle, "come wars and fightings among you? Come they not hence, even of your lusts?" The hate of a neighboring man, or neighboring nation; the lust of fame, wealth, or territory, has more than once inflamed community, arrayed man against man, nation against nation, and led to contest and bloodshed. These corrupt passions, whatever may be the scene or the extent of their influence, are the deadly foes of peace and harmony. Not only are their effects seen in street brawls, and neighborhood quarrels, but war with all its evils flows from this bitter source. Of all the evil results of man's passions, war is one of the most fearful in its details, and the most hideous in its consequences. Concealed, wreathed, garlanded, and glorified as it may be, it has seldom the shadow of an excuse. Whatever may be its "pomp or circumstance," it is usually little less than a stupendous system of robbery and murder. Aside from greater skill and talent, how is it more honest or honorable than crimes for which men are daily punished?

> "*One* murder makes the assassin's odious name,
> But *millions* damn the hero into fame."

To rob a house, or fire a dwelling, makes a villain; but to plunder kingdoms, burn cities, and slaughter nations, makes an illustrious conquerer. *That* enrolls the name among felons, *this* sends it down to future ages as immortal. O, did the spirit of true religion sway the hearts of statesmen, and control the diplomacy of nations, the bow would be broken and the spear cut in sunder, and wars would cease unto the ends of the earth. Such are some of the sources of strife in our sin-cursed world, and they serve to describe the appropriate sphere of the peace-maker. Here we mark his footsteps, and trace the effects of those Divine principles which prompt and regulate his movements in the world. To whatever department of society he may belong, whether in private or public life, in the Church or in the state, he "follows after the things which make for peace, and things whereby one may edify another."

2. *Let us now consider the mode in which he accomplishes this object.*

And it is not by the surrender of principle or the sacrifice of truth. Peace is purchased at too high a price, when a good conscience is bartered for it. He who, from fear or the love of quietude, gives up his opinions, or sides with falsehood, has neither the spirit of a man nor a Christian. Such a man can never be trusted, for such a character can only be compounded of falsehood and deceit. Compliances like these are shameful and wicked, and mark the man as a base hypocrite or a designing knave. He who can accommodate himself to all opinions, to all parties, to every side, and to each prejudice, may, in the esteem of the world, be very politic, but he is neither honest nor virtuous. Two leading objects engross the attention of the peace-maker.

The *first* is, the preservation of peace where it already exists. A conviction of its importance is always necessary to its continuance. We never care to retain what is of no value, while, on the other hand, we are willing to make any sacrifice for the preservation of what we highly esteem. Take the family circle--how important is peace to its harmony and comfort! "Where envying and strife is, there is confusion and every evil work." From such a scene gentleness and love are banished, and happiness flies to seek a more congenial home. The peaceful virtues perish, and hateful passions grow in their places. Differences arise; from these grow fierce disputes; these in turn ripen into bitter quarrels, till at last the circle is broken into fragments, and scattered abroad as so many firebrands in society. Equally important is it to communities and nations; no prosperity can attend the movements of either while disturbed by contention, or rent by discordant factions. Above all, how important in a Church! Here the loss of confidence, the want of brotherly-love, and the spirit of dissension, can only be productive of evil; they paralyze her energies, and hang like a leaden weight on her wheels; instead of achieving the conversion of sinners and the salvation of the world, she drags on heavily, or is rent in pieces by the hands of violence and strife. "The Spirit, like a peaceful dove," flies from such a scene. God does not smile upon a warring Church, and will not crown her efforts with his blessing. "Pray," says the Psalmist, "for the peace of Jerusalem; peace be within thy walls, and prosperity within thy palaces." The importance of peace is thus apparent, and an abiding conviction of this controls the peace-maker.

Next he cultivates and exhibits in his life the peaceful virtues. Regarding his character only in a negative light, the resulting benefits are at once seen and felt. He is not censorious or envious; he is no wrangler, whose element is controversy and stormy debate; he is not an evil-speaker, taking up a reproach against his neighbor, and spreading it abroad to his injury; he indulges no passion which would lead to litigation and strife; he makes war with *sin*, but not with *men*—with bad passions and corrupt desires, but not with fellow-worms. The fretful and contentious man is far more likely to create than to suppress discord; while the exercise of gentleness and charity tend directly to allay bitterness and cool the fiery passion of the heart. The peace-maker, therefore, cultivates the relations of peace with all men. The Divine command renders this imperative—"If it be possible, as much as lieth in you, live peaceably with all men." *If it be possible!* The language implies that it may be otherwise; the best of men have had their enemies, and have felt "the venomed stings of slander." For, "be thou as chaste as ice, as pure as snow, thou shalt not escape calumny." Still we are to do our utmost to preserve peace, and to appease the malice of others; we are not to begin a quarrel, but to seek peace and pursue it. Its maintenance, however, does not always depend on us. "Woe is me," says the Psalmist, "that I sojourn in Mesech, that I dwell in the tents of Kedar! My soul hath long dwelt with him that hateth peace: I am for peace;

but when I speak they are for war." We may be beset by those who oppose and persecute; they may hate religion, and slander and injure us. We are not responsible for their assaults, but we are for our conduct toward them. It may not be *possible* to prevent their unkindness to us, but it *is* possible not to quarrel with *them*, to seek peace, and evince a Christian spirit. If all Christians would do this; if they would never *provoke* to controversy; if they would injure no man by slander or unfair dealing; if they would compel none to prosecute them for want of honesty in business; if they would cease to irritate and prolong disputes, it would go far to terminate the reign of strife and restore harmony to the world.

Finally, in the preservation of peace, he refuses to listen to detraction and slander. The gossip, the tell-tale, and the defamer, are among the most dangerous members of society; they are incendiaries in the social state, whose infernal trade is to kindle and spread the flames of strife; they infest every community, and prowl through every department of life; they come by stealth into families, and excite jealousy and heart-burnings; they creep serpent-like into the Church, and it becomes a Meribah, a place of confusion and bitterness; they range through society, fomenting animosities and sowing broadcast the seeds of evil. I know of no language that can fully describe the utter meanness of backbiting and tattling; their meanness can only be equaled by their criminality. They stand in bold relief among that class of revolting crimes, for which God gave up the very heathen "to a reprobate mind," and for which they were accounted "worthy of death." "Such a man," says one of the old English prelates, "is the devil's truckman, who goes to one and buzzeth in his ear what such a one said of him, and when he hath by this means got some angry speeches from him, goes and reports them back to the other; and so by his wicked breath blows up the coals of strife between them; therefore, the proverb tells us where no wood is the fire goeth out; so, when there is no talebearer the strife ceaseth."

But it should not be forgotten that the listener shares in the guilt of him who contrives and him who retails a slander. Some, indeed, have itching ears for such reports; and though they do not make or circulate the lie, yet they are ever ready to listen, and thus to aid the scandal-monger in his unholy traffic. And if one is as ready to listen as the other is to tell, where is the difference in their guilt? Did every Christian close his ear against such gossip, and with honest indignation drive these harpies from him, it would much promote the public peace and reform this evil practice; "For as the north wind driveth away rain, so doth an angry countenance a backbiting tongue." "When both receive their reward," says an eastern proverb, "the slanderer's tongue will be nailed to the listener's ear."

His second object is, *the restoration of peace where it has been interrupted or lost.* And one method by which he does this, is an effort to reconcile contending parties. In regard to himself, if another is offended, he will cherish no improper feelings toward him, but will seek to pacify his anger; so we are taught by our Savior. "If thou bring thy gift to the altar, and there rememberest that thy brother hath aught against thee, leave there thy gift before the altar, and go thy way: first be reconciled to thy brother, and then come and offer thy gift." That is, if you have wronged him, make restitution; if you owe him a debt, pay it; if you have injured his character, confess it and ask pardon. This is both noble and heroic. If he has injured you, seek, in a gentle manner, to convince him of his wrong. There are few if any difficulties that might not at once be adjusted, if Christians would act in accordance with this sublime precept. Such is the conduct of the peace-maker in regard to others; he seeks to heal their divisions and reconcile them to each other. Inspired with love to God and man, he can not behold, without deep concern, the strifes and contentions of men—a concern which prompts a kindly interference to check the violence of passion, and reunite the alienated in friendship and love. Noble and God-like work! When shall this become the universal effort of man? Were every Christian minister and layman, every judge and lawyer, every politician and statesman to proceed upon this principle, how soon would family jars, Church disputes, vexatious lawsuits, and even national warfare, come to an end! Then men would dwell together in unity, and exulting Peace wave her olive branch over our disordered and unhappy world. It is said of Peter the Great, that he frequently surprised the magistrates by his unexpected presence in the cities of the empire. Having one day arrived at Olonez, he went first to the regency and inquired of the governor how many suits were depending in the court of chancery? "None, sire," replied the governor. "How happens that?" "*I endeavor to prevent lawsuits and conciliate the parties;* I act in such a manner that no traces of difference remain on the archives; if I am wrong, your indulgence will excuse me." "I wish," replied the Czar, "that all governors would act on your principles: go on; God and your sovereign are equally satisfied."

Promotive of the same great end, he seeks to bring men under the influences of the Gospel of Christ. This alone can eradicate the vile passions of the heart, and bless the world with peace. Religion is first pure, then peaceable. Its immediate and uniform effect is to give peace to the heart, and then to lead men to live in peace; it changes the lion into the lamb; it buries the tomahawk and scalping-knife, and unites men long separated by enmity in the embrace of a warm and holy affection. "The fruit of righteousness," says the apostle, "is sown in peace of them that make peace." The seeds of religion are not sown amid the brawling of a mob, or the tumult and thunder of battle, but amid peaceful scenes and with a peaceful spirit; and when thus sown, produce in rich abundance a harvest of peace. I repeat, religion is peace. In the heart, in society, on earth, and in heaven it is all peace. In its origin, and in all its results, it is productive only of order, goodness, and love. Happy day when the religion of the Prince of peace shall spread around the globe, and erect her throne in every heart! The earth shall then be as paradise;

wrangling and bitterness shall cease; "the shock, the shout, the groan of war," shall be unknown, and love and peace, as with a golden zone, bind all nations and all hearts together. O, with what ardent zeal and untiring effort should Christians labor for this sublime result! Continually exhibit in your life the pure and peaceful spirit of the Gospel; this alone provides a remedy for the sins and sorrows of our perishing and guilty race. Let us now consider briefly,

III. The honorable distinction of the peace-makers.

"Blessed are they," says Jesus, "*for they shall be called the children of God.*" I say honorable; and can any honor equal theirs? What are all earthly titles and preferments compared with this? "Is it a light thing," said David, when about to form an alliance to royalty, "is it a light thing to be son-in-law to the king?" And if not, what an honor is it to be a child of God, and enter the family of the King of kings! And this is no mere empty title; names with God are realities. They are called the children of God, because they are such; the name they bear is at once significant of their relationship and their nature. "They shall be called the children of God;" and in this they are distinguished from all others. They are not the children of this world, for they neither partake of its spirit nor govern themselves by its maxims; they are not the children of the wicked one, for they have renounced his authority and forsaken his service; they are the children of God. This distinction is founded upon three circumstances.

1. *They are regenerated and adopted into the Divine family.*

In our sinful estate we possess natures dissimilar to the nature of God. Besides other traits of equal malignity, we are "hateful and hating one another;" and as the child must partake of the nature of the father, so must we partake of the *Divine* nature ere we can in truth be called his children. This change in our nature is effected by the new birth; we are then born of the Spirit, born of God; and as "that which is born of the flesh is *flesh*, so that which is born of the Spirit is *spirit*." We are now brought into the family of God, "no more strangers and foreigners, but fellow-citizens with the saints, and of the household of God." The Spirit of adoption is received, the fruits of which now begin to develop themselves as the proofs of our sonship, and the essential elements of that noble character commended in this beatitude. Nothing less than this can slay the evil passions of our nature, and prepare the heart for the indwelling and supreme control of love to God and man. The mind thus renewed, finds its highest pleasure in doing good; a taste is acquired for the pursuit and enjoyment of holiness, and for the exercise of that charity which "doth not behave itself unseemly, that is not easily provoked, and that thinketh no evil."

2. *They resemble God their Father.*

This resemblance is not, indeed, perfect, but it is real; they bear his image. "The first man is of the earth, earthy; the second man is the Lord from heaven: as is the earthy, such are they also that are earthy; and as is the heavenly, such are they also that are heavenly; and as we have borne the image of the earthy, we shall also bear the image of the heavenly." Survey the Divine perfections and character; what excellence, what amiability! God is love; he is the author of peace, the very God of peace. Goodness flows from him as from a fountain, and its streams bless and beautify the universe. To the sinner he is merciful and gracious—slow to anger and of great mercy. Upon the evil and unthankful he showers his blessings, and toward his enemies he exercises long-suffering and unwearied patience. And O, when we think of his reconciling love, how he hath pursued us in our estrangement, and followed us through all tho windings and turnings of our sinful life, and sought to subdue our enmity by the tender ministries of love, even by the death of his Son, what a character does it unfold! *God* sought our reconciliation; man did not seek it; he did not desire it; it was the *offended*, not the offending party that sought peace. This, more than any thing else, shows us the Divine character, and throws around it an infinite loveliness. God is preeminently the peace-maker, and after this model is the true Christian conformed; he too is the author of peace, and his bosom swells with pure and heavenly love; he is "peaceable, gentle, easy to be entreated, full of mercy and good fruits, without partiality and without hypocrisy." Like him who sends rain and sunbeams on the evil and the good, he is merciful "after his power," doing good to all men; he is patient and slow to wrath, tender-hearted and forgiving. Clothed with meek humility, he goes about doing good. From a heart of love he dispenses peace and joy; and from a character rich in resemblance to all that is benevolent and holy, emits a pure and steady light. In a word, he embodies in his life the precept of the apostle, "Do all things without murmurings and disputings: that ye may be blameless and harmless, the sons of God, without rebuke, in the midst of a crooked and perverse nation, among whom ye shine as lights in the world."

3. *Their conduct.*

The conduct becoming a child is obedience; and such a course always calls forth the regards and acknowledgments of the father. One of the most striking characteristics of the peace-maker, as a child of God, is obedience. His course of life, compared with the law of God and the precepts of the Gospel, furnishes the evidence. His principles of action, his amiable disposition of heart, his lovely traits of character, his benevolent and God-like actions, are all in beautiful harmony with their demands. He employs his time, his talents, his influence, in wise and zealous efforts to bless mankind, and promote the glory of God. As a child, he *loves* the service of God; here "labor is rest, and pain is sweet." Amid self-denial and toil, reproach and suffering, he can say, "My *meat* is to do the will of Him that sent me, and to finish his work." Children of God! What a distinction, what a privilege! "For if children, then heirs: heirs of God and joint-heirs with Christ." How high their destiny, how splendid their inheritance—a crown; a kingdom, "incorruptible, undefiled, and that fadeth not away!"

Permit me now to commend this character to your study and imitation. Scipio, we are told in history, declared that he was inflamed with a virtuous and heroic spirit, by contemplating the statues of his ancestors. But here is a character infinitely superior, not sculptured in breathless marble, or molded after earthly patterns, but fashioned like the Son of God, and inspired with his life and spirit. It is hardly possible to think of the amiable tempers of the peace-maker, without an ardent desire to possess them. What a revolution would their presence make in your heart! "Instead of the thorn, the fig-tree would come up, and instead of the brier, should come up the myrtle-tree; you should then go out with joy, and be led forth with peace." The malignant demons of hate, malice, and revenge, would then be driven from your heart, and the bright angels of love, and peace, and gentleness, would descend to rest and abide in your bosom. Then would God own you as his child; his name would be written in your forehead, and his image would shine in your holy and beneficent life. "God," says Luther, "dwells not in Babylon, which is confusion; but in Salem, which is peace. There he has recorded his name; there he has fixed the mercy-seat; there he himself delights to dwell." Who can contemplate the mild benevolence of Melancthon, the angelic meekness of Fletcher, the conciliating gentleness of Summerfield, without a glow of desire to be like them, and without perceiving how much such dispositions would contribute to the peace and harmony of mankind?

In the formation of this character, meditation and

prayer are all-important. With what profound attention does the artist study his model! So must you long and deeply ponder this character. Invoke Divine assistance; pray for light and guidance; pray that love to God and man may fill and control your heart. The celebrated Boerhaave was remarkable for his humility, gentleness, and expansive charity. A friend inquired how he had acquired such a character? He replied, "I am naturally warm and irritable, but have been enabled by daily meditation and prayer to subdue my heat of temper." Pray for large measures of the Spirit. How sweet to learn from such a teacher! How easy to cultivate these tempers with his almighty aid! Unspeakably benign and purifying is the agency of that divine Sanctifier on our dark and sinful hearts. Behold the restored demoniac—no longer mangling his own flesh, or assaulting with rage and fury the unsuspecting traveler, but calmly sitting at the feet of Jesus, his face radiant with joy, his heart swelling with peace and love! Such shall you become under God's transforming power. O, begin this sublime pursuit; let it be your high and constant aim to attain the character of the peace-maker, who,

"While he lives,
Knows no bliss but that which virtue gives,
And when he dies, bequeaths a lofty name,
A light, a landmark on the cliffs of fame."

LECTURE IX.

EIGHTH BEATITUDE.

"Blessed are they which are persecuted for righteousness' sake: for theirs is the kingdom of heaven. Blessed are ye when men shall revile you, and persecute you, and shall say all manner of evil against you falsely, for my sake. Rejoice, and be exceeding glad: for great is your reward in heaven: for so persecuted they the prophets which were before you." MATTHEW v, 10–12.

THE way to heaven is beset with difficulty and danger. Self-denials are to be made, crosses are to be taken up, and tribulations to be endured. These are inevitable to a life of piety. "If any man," says Jesus, "will be my disciple, let him deny himself and take up his cross daily, and follow me." The path he trod was the path of sorrow. It led through scenes of temptation, toil, and suffering; and he who would follow the Savior must expect to pass through the same or similar perils. It is enough that the servant be as his Lord. This, to multitudes, is a source of deep discouragement. It is often hard enough, with a clear sky and favoring gales, to breast the tide of corrupt nature: how much more when the sky is overspread with clouds, and the tempest rages, and the billows roll! Then it is that many become offended with religion, and fall away, and hasten to leave a course charged with so many difficulties. This liability to discouragement we have all felt. It has been the experience of the wisest and the best. We have become disheartened in duty; we have shrunk from self-denial and the cross; we have fainted in the day of opposition and adversity. Like the pilgrims in their progress to the heavenly city, we would fain exchange the rough and narrow path for the green and easy by-ways on either side. But it should never be forgotten, that the path of duty is the path of safety; and that they who forsake it for other ways shall be snared in an evil net, and perish the victims of their own presumption.

On no subject has our Savior spoken more fully or more tenderly than that to which we have just alluded. He foresaw our discouragements and sought to remove them. To counteract despondency, and inspire hope; to repress the alarms of fear, and nerve the heart with faith and courage, he uttered the most cheering promises. Despair itself should kindle into hope, and feebleness rise with immortal energy under his inspiring words.

As we have intimated, duty, sacrifice, and suffering are intimately connected with a profession of religion. They have their respective discouragements, the force of which we daily feel; and it is cheering, indeed, to look over those precious promises from which the pious in all ages have drawn encouragement and strength. Look, for example, at the duty of prayer. In this we often faint and grow weary. But says the Savior, "Ask, and ye *shall* receive; seek, and ye *shall* find; knock, and it *shall* be opened unto you." Who can doubt, when such assurances are heard from the lips of Truth? Do we shrink from the sacrifice religion demands? His language is, "There is no man that hath left houses, or brethren, or sisters, or father, or mother, or wife, or children, or lands, for my sake and the Gospel's, but shall receive an hundred-fold now in this time, and in the world to come eternal life." Are we hated of men and persecuted for his sake? How consolatory are his words, "Blessed are ye when men shall revile you, and persecute you, and shall say all manner of evil against you falsely, for my sake. Rejoice, and be exceeding glad: for great is your reward in heaven!" These are the words which, in other times, have inspired the timid with more than mortal courage, and made them "struggle with the martyr for the stake, and bless heaven for the flames."

"Blessed are they which are persecuted for righteousness' sake." "To persecute," says a recent expositor, "means literally to pursue, to follow after, as one does a flying enemy. Here it means to vex or oppress one on account of his religion." Hence, to injure another in his feelings, reputation, or property, or to endanger or take away his life for the sake of his religious opinions or conduct, is persecution. The Savior predicted that such would be the lot of all his disciples. "In the world," said he, "ye shall have tribulation;" "If they have persecuted me, they will also persecute you. They shall put you out of the synagogues; yea, the time cometh, that whosoever killeth you, will think that he doeth God service. And the brother shall deliver up the brother to death, and the father the child: and the children shall rise up against their parents and cause them to be put to death." We may, therefore, regard persecution as inevitable. In some form or other it *will* befall the followers of Christ. I invite your attention,

I. To THE VARIOUS FORMS OF PERSECUTION.

And we may regard them as three-fold.

1. *Persecution by secret malignity and hate.*

This is the lowest form of persecution; but it has, nevertheless, a most decided character. Thus it has existed ever since the human heart became depraved, and will never cease to exist till divine grace completely renovates the human soul. The carnal mind is enmity against God. It stands in direct and unyielding conflict with his nature and his laws. All, therefore, who bear his image and partake of his nature, become the objects of dislike, if not of hate. This enmity may be unseen, but it is not the less real. No utterance of the lip, no change of the countenance may indicate its presence; but it is there hidden far down in the depths of the heart, a stern and stubborn principle, that can not be subjected to the Divine will. Its manifestation, in the form of persecution, is frequently alluded to by our blessed Lord: "Ye shall be *hated* of all men for my name's sake. If the world *hate* you, ye know that it *hated* me before it hated you. If ye were of the world, the world would love its own; but because ye are not of the world, therefore the world *hateth* you." From this principle every overt act of persecution has arisen, and its violent outbreaks are only prevented by the restraints which a merciful Providence has interposed. Self-respect, interest, the force of public sentiment, and legal provisions may all have their influence; but the primary check arises from Him who holds the reins of universal government, and who says to the enemies of Christ, as well as the mighty ocean waves, "Hitherto shalt thou come, but no further; and here shall thy proud waves be staid."

Some may perhaps doubt whether they possess such a spirit; but if they will honestly examine their hearts, and the views and feelings they entertain upon this subject, they will perhaps see that I have not gone too far in my statements; they will find that very enmity of which I have spoken, like a spreading leprosy, infecting every power of the soul; they will discover a strong dislike to the claims of God's law and the holiness he so urgently demands; they will find the same distaste to holiness in his people. They wish they were less strict and less conscientious, more liberal in their views and more conformed to the world in their actions. They feel that if they were more devoted to pleasure and plans of gain; if they would be companions at the gay party, at the theater and the ball-room, they would like them better. Their spirit and example is a reproof and a rebuke; and though no impropriety of speech may betray their settled dislike, yet they feel a fire in their bosoms, the flames of which they find it sometimes difficult to repress. Now, this is the spirit of persecution, the very same dark and fiend-like spirit which, more than once, has drenched the earth with righteous blood.

2. *Persecutions by open reproach and opposition.* The heart's inward hate finds an easy outlet through the lips. Cruel words and bitter taunts are its natural language, and often uttered by those who despise the way of truth. The persecutions of our

Savior furnish an instance. Thus they said of him that he was a Samaritan—a term of the highest reproach; that he was mad and had a devil. They called him a wine-bibber; a friend and companion of wicked men. And when that pure and holy being hung bleeding upon the cross, they bitterly reproached him, and, amid the agonies of death, reviled and mocked him. Similar treatment he predicted would befall his people in succeeding ages. "If," said he, "they have called the master of the house Beelzebub, much more will they call them of his household. The disciple is not above his master, nor the servant above his Lord." And to prepare them for these scenes of reproach he says, "Blessed are ye when men shall revile you, and shall say all manner of evil against you falsely, for my sake." The time was approaching when they would need these encouragements. They were soon to become the objects of derision and scorn. Erelong men would pursue them with bitter hate and furious opposition, persecuting them even unto strange cities. Amid the overwhelming scenes of Pentecost, when, if ever, the enemies of Christ should have been hushed to silence, they mocked and ridiculed. Similar has been the conduct of wicked men in every age, to stigmatize religion and check its progress in the world. Under the reign of Domitian, one of the early Roman emperors, the most absurd and wicked tales were invented to blast the reputation of Christians. They were accused of meeting together for the grossest immorality—of murdering their children and feasting upon their bodies. They were charged with sedition and rebellion; and as often as any calamity befell the empire, as earthquakes, pestilence, or famine, it was attributed to their impiety. In modern times they have been reviled as fools and fanatics. Ill names and odious epithets have been heaped upon them. The names of Huguenot, Puritan, Quaker, and Methodist were first given in derision, and still perpetuate the memory of sufferings borne for the sake of Christ.

Even at present the same means are employed to prevent a profession of religion or compel its abandonment. Many thus suffer; and the trial is sometimes but little less severe than the infliction of bodily pain. Let a young man, for instance, launch out into a gay and reckless life; let him figure amid scenes of pleasure and dissipation, neglecting God, despising the Savior, and scoffing at religion, and he receives the smiles and applause of all his companions in folly. But let that same young man become thoughtful and serious; let him forsake his former associates in vice, and connect himself with the Church of Christ, and at once they begin to deride him. One points the finger of scorn, another brands him with an ill name, and the whole company make him the butt of jest and ridicule. Alas! how many have surrendered their profession and left the paths of virtue to escape the revilings of a godless world!

Authority and power are sometimes exerted in opposition to religion. Parents oppose their children, husbands their wives, and wives their husbands. Persecution from those we venerate and love; who have the highest earthly claim to our obedience, but whose claims conflict with duty to God, constitutes one of the severest forms of trial. Do I address one thus situated? You ask, What shall I do? I answer, obey God. But I am a child, and owe obedience to my parents. True, but we must obey God *rather* than man. If need be, sacrifice all for Christ. Perhaps he may make you the honored instrument in the conversion of your parents. A large and irreligious family resided a few miles from the city of New York. The father and mother were stern opposers of religion. It so happened that a little daughter of these parents became connected with a Sunday school, and was soon deeply interested in the instruction she received. When the father heard of it he forbade her going again; but the little girl, supposing he was not in earnest, continued to go. At length the father, mother, brothers, and sisters threatened to turn her out of doors if she went again. When the next Sunday morning came the little girl dressed herself as usual, except putting on her bonnet. When the hour for Sunday school arrived she went to her father, and, taking him by the hand, said, "Father, I love *you*, but I love *Jesus better;* so now I bid you farewell." She then took leave of her mother, brothers, and sisters in the same way, and left them for the school. Her conduct touched a tender chord in the father's hard heart. He said nothing, but silently followed her to the school, went in and at once became interested. The next Sunday he persuaded his wife to accompany him; she, too, was won. Soon the whole family entered the school and then the Church, of which they became active and devoted members. Little did this angel child imagine that God would make her the happy means of leading that family to the Savior of the world.

Husbands sometimes oppose and persecute their wives. That tender, trustful, and devoted woman would secure her salvation. For this she is annoyed and even persecuted with cruel threats by him who bears the holy name of husband. The following incident, related by Dr. Baird, will illustrate this conduct: "A few years since a lady, the wife of a wealthy citizen, became deeply interested in her salvation. Her husband, who was an infidel, violently opposed her. At length she became a decided Christian. He then told her if she went to the chapel again he would take her life. Knowing well his character, and believing he would execute his threat, she called upon her minister to ask his advice. 'I know not,' said he, 'what to say, but we will pray to God for wisdom.' They kneeled and prayed. She arose from her knees, and, without saying a word, returned home. The next Sabbath she was found in the chapel, worshiping as if for the last time. At the close of the service she returned, and, entering the house, met her husband. 'Have you been to the chapel?' said he. 'Yes.' 'Did I not tell you that I would kill you if you went again? How dare you to go?' She meekly replied, 'I must obey God rather than man.' He hesitated. Perceiving this she said, 'Why do you intend to kill me? Have I been a worse wife to you, a worse mother to your children, since I became a Christian?' 'No,' said he, letting the weapon fall from his hand; 'no, and I promise never to oppose you again. Will you pray for me?' They bowed in prayer together, and that husband became a decided and humble follower of the Lamb."

3. *Persecution by the infliction of pains and penalties.*

Living, as we do, under a form of government where the rights of conscience are both admitted and respected, we can scarcely realize that Christians have been called to suffer in this manner. We sit under our own vine and fig tree; none dare to molest or make us afraid. The glorious eagle of American independence spreads his protecting wings over our religious as well as our civil liberties, thanks to a benignant Providence. And long may they be preserved from the vandal hands of bigotry and the burning hate of priest-ridden fanaticism! But there have been times when men, for their religion, "had the trial of cruel mockings and scourgings, yea, moreover, of bonds and imprisonments: they were stoned, they were sawn asunder, were tempted, were slain with the sword: they wandered in sheep-skins and goat-skins; being destitute, afflicted, tormented." The murderous crusades against the primitive Christians and the Waldenses; the atrocious massacres of England, Ireland, and France; and the dungeons, the racks and fires of the Inquisition, are melancholy demonstration of this. Persecution in this form has arisen principally from three sources—the Jews, Pagan and Papal Rome.

The Jews stand as the first enemies of Christianity, and the first persecutors of Christians. The Son of God himself fell a victim to their malice. After his death almost every form of cruelty which their mad zeal could invent was inflicted upon the apostles and the infant Church. Extermination was their watchword. St. Stephen was the first who suffered for the testimony of Jesus, and stands before us crowned with the honor of leading the van of that glorious band of Christian martyrs which soon followed. Within the brief period comprehended in the Acts of the Apostles, thousands perished by violence, and thousands more suffered by "the spoiling of their goods," by imprisonment, by scourging and banishment. Filled with rage against the followers of Him they had crucified, they breathed out threatenings and slaughter against all who dared to assume the name of the hated Nazarene. The effect of this was to scatter the disciples abroad. But wherever they went they preached Jesus. The Gospel was thus rapidly diffused, and converts multiplied. They spread over the Roman empire, and were found even in the household of Cæsar. The purity of their lives and their unyielding opposition to the idolatries of heathenism, aroused the spirit of persecution, and *Pagan Rome* raised her iron arm to crush the followers of Jesus. History records ten general persecutions under the Roman emperors. The reigns of Nero, Domitian, Trajan, Decius, Dioclesian, and others during the first four centuries, were distinguished for their fierce opposition and barbaric cruelty to the saints of God. Some were scourged to death, and others were slain by the sword or thrown into the sea. Some were covered with the skins of wild beasts, and torn in pieces by furious dogs. Others were wrapped in combustible garments and fastened on crosses, and at night set on fire to illuminate the cities where they suffered. During the reign of the monster Dioclesian, seventeen thousand, it is said, were slain in one month. In a single province of the empire one hundred and fifty-four thousand Christians perished by violence, besides seven hundred thousand who suffered banishment and other cruel inflictions. Among those who received the crown of martyrdom, during this bloody period, we find the illustrious names of Ignatius, Bishop of Antioch, and Polycarp, Bishop of Smyrna. Ignatius, having boldly defended the faith before the Emperor Adrian, was thrown into prison and tormented in the most shocking manner. After being scourged, he was compelled to hold coals of fire in his hands, and papers dipped in oil were put to his sides and set on fire. His flesh was then torn with red-hot pincers, and at last he was dispatched by wild beasts. Polycarp, being arrested, was brought before the proconsul, and condemned to be burnt in the market-place. Having been bound to the stake, he was besought to abjure Christ. The venerable saint replied, "Eighty and six years have I served Jesus, and he never did me harm; why then should I renounce him?" The fagots were then lighted, and his body consumed to ashes.

But cruel as the persecutions of the heathen were, they have been outdone by those bearing the hallowed name of Christian. *Papal Rome* stands before the world with the enviable distinction of having reduced persecution to a science and a profession, and in the arts of refined cruelty and savage barbarity outrivaling all her predecessors. In tracing the history of the persecutions of the Church of Rome, how easy is it to identify this power with the woman of the Apocalypse, "clothed in purple and scarlet color, and decked with gold and precious stones; drunk with the blood of the saints, and with the blood of the martyrs of Jesus!" "How applicable this is to the Papacy," says a recent writer, "let the blood shed in the valleys of Piedmont; the blood shed in the low countries by the Duke of Alva; the blood shed on St. Bartholomew's day; and the blood shed in the Inquisition testify."

Taking for our stand-point the era of the reformation under Martin Luther, a scene of cruelty and suffering spreads out before the eye unparalleled in the annals of the world. The Reformation was distinguished by its love for the Bible, and its opposition to the errors and ambition of Romanism. It was scarcely born ere the Pope and his clergy marshaled their forces for its destruction. Anathematized and excommunicated, the friends of true religion were pursued and hunted like beasts of prey; and for nearly half a century parts of Germany, Bohemia, Poland, and Hungary, were drenched with Protestant blood. The Inquisition erected by the popes, especially for the detection and punishment of heretics, was at this period set to work with greater efficiency; and under the triple sway of ignorance, superstition, and bigotry, it became one of the most frightful engines of persecution ever employed against the saints of God. The horrid scenes enacted within its gloomy dungeons, where, without distinction of age or sex, Christians were flayed alive, roasted in brazen pans, and broken on wheels and racks, stun the imagination and shock every feeling of humanity. The best blood of Italy, Spain, and Portugal has been shed to glut the appetite of this infamous tribunal.

In the British isles Protestant blood has flowed like water. Thousands of whom the world was not worthy, having witnessed a good profession, laid down their lives "for the word of God and for the testimony of Jesus." The reign of Queen Mary forms a gloomy epoch in history. Her weak mind, her bigotry, superstition, and cruelty, made her a fit instrument of priestly intolerance; and faithfully did they employ her in wearing out the saints of God. Among the vast numbers who suffered unto death, the names of Hooper, Taylor, Latimer, Ridley, and Cranmer, Archbishop of Canterbury, shine illustriously upon the pages of English martyrology.

"But no country," in the language of history, "has produced more martyrs than France." In this beautiful land the demon of persecution has literally rioted in the blood of the saints. The Waldenses were among the first victims of intolerant law and Popish cruelty. They were a pious and holy people, chiefly inhabiting the valleys of Piedmont. Their refusal to receive the errors of Romanism drew upon them all the fury of the Church. No language can describe their sufferings, or picture the atrocious cruelties inflicted upon them. The sad story of their wrongs, for Christ's sake, might well be doubted, were it not the utterance of impartial and authentic history. Early in the sixteenth century we find a large body of evangelical Christians in France. They are known in history as the

Huguenots. The sufferings of these people have scarcely a parallel in the history of religion. In the massacre of Bartholomew alone, seventy thousand were butchered in cold blood. This wholesale murder, enough to damn a nation, was headed by a fiend in woman's shape—Catharine de Medicis, the mother of Charles the Ninth, and a bigoted Papist. Upon the revocation of the edict of Nantz, by Louis XIV, one of the most infamous of modern princes, a terrific storm burst upon the French Protestants. Thousands were murdered in various ways, the prisons were filled to suffocation, and fifty thousand were driven into banishment. Here we must pause. But who can hear even this brief recital without dropping a tear over the sufferings of the saints, and the madness and depravity of their enemies? It has been computed, from authentic data, that more than *fifty millions* of Protestants have fallen victims to Papal bigotry and superstition. How long, O Lord, holy and true, dost thou not judge and avenge thy saints on them that dwell on the earth! But the plans of Providence are hastening to maturity, and the day of vengeance is at hand. Let us now briefly advert

II. To THE REASON OF THEIR PERSECUTIONS—"*For righteousness' sake.*"

Because they are righteous—because they are the friends of God and the disciples of Jesus. St. Paul expresses the same thing in different language: "Yea, and all that will live godly in Christ Jesus, shall suffer persecution." It is important to guard this point; for it is only when we suffer for righteousness' sake, or for Christ's sake, that we may apply the consolations of this passage to our hearts. In the language of St. Peter, a man may suffer as a murderer, or as a thief, or as an evil-doer, or as a busy-body in other men's matters. Now, thus to suffer is not persecution, but simple justice. "A man may embrace some absurd opinion and call it *religion;* he may adopt a ludicrous style of dress, from the mere love of singularity, and call it *conscience;* or he may be boorish in his manners and rude in his deportment, outraging all the laws of social life, and call *this deadness to the world;* and for these he may be ridiculed and laughed at; but let him not infer, therefore, that he is a Christian, and that he is to be enrolled among the martyrs." It is only when he suffers for *doing right*, for an honest effort to *obey God*, that he is entitled to blessings of the persecuted.

The righteous are distinguished by their adherence to the truth as it is in Jesus—not the teachings of men or the traditions of the Church, but the simple truth of the Gospel. This they have chosen as their heritage forever, and for this they are willing to sacrifice every thing. It was "for the *word of God* and for the *testimony of Jesus*," that the ancient worthies laid down their lives. Rather than surrender the BIBLE, millions of Protestants have cheerfully poured out their hearts' blood. They are distinguished by the spirituality of their experience. Salvation by faith, a felt and living reality in the heart, forms its chief element. From this flows love to God, deadness to the world, heavenly-mindedness, and joy in the Holy Ghost. This experience sustained the "confessors" with almighty energy in their fight of afflictions, when they resisted unto blood striving against sin. They are distinguished by their practical godliness. In them we see displayed the humility of the poor in spirit, the gentleness of the meek, the kindness of the merciful, and the benevolence of the peace-maker. Their life is the embodiment of the Divine law. They walk even as Christ walked, reflecting, in brilliant light, the holy life and example of the Son of God. Like him, "when reviled they reviled not again, when persecuted they threatened not; but, suffering according to the will of God, they commit the keeping of their souls to him as unto a faithful Creator." But can these characters be the objects of reproach and scorn, of bitter hate and shameful indignity? Why, what evil have they done? Are they not pure, and holy, and harmless? And yet the appalling fact is before us, that the wisest and the best of our race have thus suffered. The devoted and self-sacrificing Paul, the amiable and Christ-like John, and even the immaculate Son of God were reviled and cruelly entreated. Two reasons may be assigned for this:

1. *One arises out of the depravity of the human heart.*

The consequence of this is opposition to God. And further, this depraved heart is controlled by the prince of evil—the enemy of all righteousness. "He works in the children of disobedience," producing hardness of heart, blindness of mind, and a still stronger hostility of will to God. Between those who serve God and those who serve him not, there is a wide and palpable difference. The one is of the spirit, the other of the flesh. And as "he that was born of the flesh persecuted him that was born of the Spirit," even so it is at present. The first walks according to godliness, the latter "according to the course of this world;" and thus walking, says the apostle, "they think it strange that ye run not with them to the same excess of riot, speaking evil of you." The Savior, assigning the reason of persecution, says, "If ye were of the world, the world would love its own; but because ye are not of the world, therefore the world hateth you." "The reason," says Mr. Wesley, "is plain. The spirit which is in the world is directly hostile to the spirit which is of God. It must, therefore, be, that those who are of the world will stand opposed to them who are of God. There is the utmost contrariety between them in all their opinions, desires, and tempers, and hitherto the leopard and the kid can not lie down in peace together." Between good and evil there is no affinity, and can be no agreement. Evil, through its proper agents, has ever sought to crush and exterminate the good. Abel, slain by his brother's hand, was but a sad prelude to the fearful contest—slain because his own works were righteous and his brother's evil.

2. *A second reason arises out of the Divine permission.*

I use the word permission here in the lowest possible sense. God is not only a sovereign, but the friend and father of his people, and without his permission no enemy can hurt or destroy them. He who laid the foundations of the earth, and shut in the sea with bars and doors, hath set bounds to their malice and fixed a limit over which they can not pass. But why, you ask, does God permit these sufferings to befall his people? Without an attempt to fathom his designs, or assign all the reasons of his conduct, may they not, under the Divine blessing, promote the highest interests of the Christian, and eminently conduce to the perfection of his character? The Scriptures warrant this view. Thus they are sometimes intended to test the faith of Christians. St. Peter refers to this when he says, "If need be ye are in heaviness through manifold temptations: that the *trial of your faith*, being much more precious than of gold that perisheth, though it be tried with fire, might be found unto praise, and honor, and glory at the appearing of Jesus Christ." This is necessary. There is much in the world that passes for religion, which has only to be *tested* in order to discover its true character. Like spurious coin, it bears the external mark of genuineness; but when the test is applied it is found to be counterfeit and worthless. Persecutions and trials have a salutary effect upon Christian graces. Summer suns ripen and mellow the fruit, and sufferings sanctified hasten spiritual maturity. They furnish occasions for their exercise, and the aliment proper to their growth and healthfulness. Under such circumstances he can show his love to God. He can exhibit the sublime achievement of overcoming evil with good. He can love his enemies and pray for those that despitefully use and persecute him. Patience, meekness, and love, those superior traits of Christian character, can here display themselves as no where else in the ordinary scenes of human life. "The Christian," says one, "is like those flowers that best effuse their odors when bruised. He is like the firmament, and it is the darkness of affliction that makes his starry graces shine forth." They minister to greater purity of life and greater devotedness to God. "No chastening," says the apostle, "for the present seemeth to be joyous but grievous: nevertheless, afterward it yieldeth the peaceable fruit of righteousness unto them which are exercised thereby." St. Paul speaks of this as a *universal* truth, and it is so. There is no Christian that is not benefited by his trials. When the storm has passed away, and, sometimes, while it rages, he is able to say, it was *good for me to be afflicted;* and when he has reached the final hour, and comes to lay his head upon the pillow of death, he can look back and see the effects of these trials. They have strengthened his graces; they have shed their hallowing influence over his heart, and scattered their golden fruit all along the path of his earthly pilgrimage. Let us now observe,

III. THE SPIRIT IN WHICH THESE PERSECUTIONS ARE TO BE RECEIVED.

And it is the spirit of holy joy. "Rejoice," says the Savior, "and be exceeding glad;" and this is the feeling every-where recommended as proper to them who suffer for Christ's sake. "My brethren," says St. James, "count it all *joy* when ye fall into divers temptations." "If ye suffer for righteousness' sake," in the language of St. Peter, "*happy* are ye; and be not afraid of their terror, neither be troubled." Though persecutions may seem formidable, and even terrific, yet let no apprehension of danger trouble you. If a true Christian, you have no reason to fear. God is your protector, and he is able to roll back every mountain wave, to vanquish every foe, and crown you with present and eternal triumph. And "if any man," says the same apostle, "suffer as a Christian, let him not be ashamed; but let him *glorify* God on this behalf." But is this possible? Can men take joyfully the reproaches of the wicked, the spoiling of their goods, or a cruel death by martyrdom? They can. When, on one occasion, the apostles were arraigned before the council and sorely beaten, they were sent away, charged to preach no more in the name of Jesus. But how did they feel under their sufferings? Why, they departed from the council *rejoicing* "that they were counted worthy to suffer shame for Christ." See two of these apostles in the dungeons of Philippi. Though suffering every indignity, though lacerated and bleeding, yet the midnight hour is vocal, and those gloomy walls resound with their prayers to God, and hymns of grateful joy. A religion that can thus raise and support the heart under trial *must* be divine. "Rejoice and be exceeding glad!" Two reasons are assigned for this:

1. *These sufferings identify them with the worthies of every age.*

"For so persecuted they the prophets which were before you." The Savior intimates, in another place, that righteous blood had been shed in every age, from Abel down to Zechariah, who was slain between the porch and the altar. To these saints of olden time St. Paul alludes when he says, "Some had the trial of cruel mockings and scourgings, yea, moreover, of bonds and imprisonments. They were stoned, they were sawn asunder, they were slain with the sword." To these millions have since been added—the apostles, and martyrs, and the early reformers. What a brilliant company!—like an unbroken line of light, stretching from the first age of the world down to our own times! With these noble men, of whom the world was not worthy, every suffering Christian becomes identified. He takes rank with them in the cause of the Redeemer—the cause in which they toiled and triumphed. They bear the marks of Christ—noble scars, received in the glorious conflict of truth and right. "From henceforth," says the veteran Paul, "let no man trouble *me*, for I bear in my body the marks of the Lord Jesus." It can scarcely be doubted but that he here refers to the marks of stripes and sufferings received in the service of Christ. He had often been scourged. He bore the wales on his person then. They were *sacred* scars, connecting him with the worthies of other times and with the cause of Christ, in which he suffered. It is said that Lafayette, when struck in the foot by a musket-ball at Germantown, exclaimed, "I prize this wound as among the most valued of my honors." And why? Because he then took rank with the patriots of every age and nation. That wound identified him forever with the sacred cause of human liberty. So of every Christian. If it has not been his privilege to suffer like Paul, yet he should bear *some* mark; something that may stand as an evidence of his love to Christ. This will introduce him to the noble company of the saints, and invest him with an honor that no ducal crown or kingly diadem can confer.

2. *They are entitled to a glorious recompense above.*

"For great is your reward in heaven." Among all the crowns of heaven, the martyr's crown is the brightest."

> "Who are these arrayed in white,
> Brighter than the noonday sun?
> *Foremost* of the sons of light;
> *Nearest* the eternal throne?
> These are they that bore the cross;
> Nobly for their Master stood;
> Sufferers in his righteous cause;
> Followers of their Savior God."

Their faithful testimony and their sufferings for Christ will exalt them to the loftiest seats of heavenly bliss. Having come out of great tribulation they stand near the throne, clad in robes of white, bearing the symbol of victory in their hands, and the symbol of regal honor on their heads. They toil no more, they suffer no more, they weep no more. Under the inspiration of this promise many of the early Christians *sought* to become martyrs. They literally rejoiced and leaped for joy at the prospect of death for the sake of Jesus, "knowing that these light afflictions, which are but for a moment, work for us *a far more exceeding and eternal weight of glory.*" "Beloved," says St. Paul, himself a martyr, "think it not strange concerning the fiery trial which is sent to try you, as though some strange thing happened unto you; but *rejoice*, inasmuch as ye are partakers of Christ's sufferings; that when his glory shall be revealed, ye may be glad also with exceeding joy." When the celebrated Jerome of Prague was bound to the stake, and the executioner was about to kindle the fire *behind* him, he said, "Bring thy torch hither, and do thine office *before* my face: had I feared death I might have avoided it." As the fagots began to blaze, he commenced singing in a loud voice, and continued to rejoice till suffocated in the flames. When that apostolic man, George Wishart, was brought to the stake, he exclaimed, "For the true Gospel I suffer this day with a *glad* heart. Behold and consider my countenance—ye shall not see me change color—I fear not this fire. My faith is such that I know surely *that my soul shall drink new wine with my Savior this night in his kingdom.*" His body was then consumed to ashes, but his soul, wafted on wings of fire, soared to its appointed throne above.

CONCLUSION.

1. Are any of you called to suffer for Christ's sake? Do friends reproach and oppose you? Think it not strange; but rejoice that you are counted worthy to suffer in a cause so glorious. It is a hallowed cause; it is the cause of your Redeemer, in which millions have toiled, and suffered, and bled. Evince a Christian spirit. Be patient and forgiving. "Avenge not yourselves, neither give place unto wrath. Commit the keeping of your souls to God in *well-doing* as unto a faithful Creator." The day of your redemption draws nigh. See the crown; it gleams and flashes with immortal glory. Hold that fast which thou hast, though earth and hell should beset thy pathway; "for I reckon that the sufferings of the present time are not worthy to be compared with the glory that shall be revealed in us."

2. Let me utter a note of warning to the persecutor. How dishonorable and impious is your oppo-

sition to the cause of God! But are there such now? There are. All who would in any way deter others from a profession of religion are persecutors. True, the more violent forms of persecution are at present unknown. · But Christians still hear their names vilified, their opinions abused, and their Redeemer blasphemed; and often are their feelings rudely torn by the cutting sarcasm and the bitter sneer. In these and a variety of ways they are still subjected to shame for the sake of Christ, and they should expect it. But let the persecutor remember that the eye of God is on him, and that the prayers and tears, it may be, of a wife or child, cry to heaven with a martyr's pleading. Let him remember that their Redeemer is mighty, and that he will show himself strong to avenge the innocent and punish the oppressor. Ay, let him remember that his opposition must end in ruin—bitter and eternal ruin. Awful and sudden judgments have sometimes swept persecutors away in the midst of their days, the very fires of hell breaking forth before their time, to torment and devour them. O beware! beware! Cease, I beseech you, to fight against God! Ground your weapons; repent of thy wickedness; seek pardon of God; embrace the Gospel, and walk with us in the way to heaven. Take up your cross and follow Christ. We can not secure you from privation or promise you exemption from suffering; but we will promise that you shall share in the songs, and crowns, and thrones of them who have overcome "by the blood of the Lamb, and by the word of their testimony."